PROCLAIMING PENTECOST

100 SERMON OUTLINES ON THE POWER OF THE HOLY SPIRIT

MARK R. TURNEY
EDITOR

DENZIL R. MILLER
ASSOCIATE EDITOR

A DECADE OF PENTECOST PUBLICATION

Proclaiming Pentecost: 100 Sermon Outlines on the Power of the Holy Spirit. © 2011, AIA Publications. All rights reserved. No part of this book may be reproduced, stored in a retrieval system, or transmitted in any form or by any means—electronic, mechanical, photocopy, recording, or otherwise—without prior written permission of the copyright owner, except brief quotations used in connection with reviews in magazines or newspapers.

All Scripture quotations in this book, unless otherwise indicated, are from the HOLY BIBLE, NEW INTERNATIONAL VERSION. Copyright © 1973, 1978, 1984 by International Bible Society. Used by permission.

Library of Congress Cataloging-in-Publication Data
Turney, Mark R., 1968–
Miller, Denzil R., 1946–
Proclaiming Pentecost: 100 Sermon Outlines on the Power of the Holy Spirit / Mark R. Turney / Denzil R. Miller

ISBN: 978-0-7361-0452-4

1. Bible. 2. Practical Theology: Homiletics. 4. Pentecostal. 5. Holy Spirit. 6. Missions

Printed in the United States of America
AIA Publications, Springfield, MO, USA
2011

A Decade of Pentecost Publication
Websites: www.DecadeofPentecost.org
                  www.ActsinAfrica.org

Contents

Contents 3
Sermon Author Index 7
Foreword 10
Introduction 12

SECTION 1 – THE BAPTISM IN THE HOLY SPIRIT 15

   1. The Acts 1:8 Promise of Jesus 16
   2. The Baptism in the Holy Spirit 18
   3. The Baptism in the Holy Spirit Is What We Need 20
   4. Baptism in the Holy Spirit Series 22
   5. Baptism in the Holy Spirit Series 24
   6. Baptism in the Holy Spirit Series 26
   7. Baptism in the Holy Spirit Series 28
   8. The Comforter Has Come 30
   9. Common Questions About the Baptism in the Holy Spirit 32
  10. The Day of Pentecost 34
  11. Did You Receive the Spirit When You Believed? 36
  12. Don't Leave Home Without It 38
  13. Fan Into Flame the Gift of God 40
  14. Have You Received Since You Believed? 42
  15. The Holy Spirit Empowers 44
  16. Jesus' Personal Instructions on Receiving the Spirit 46
  17. Jesus, the Baptizer in the Holy Spirit 47
  18. Jesus, Savior and Baptizer 48
  19. Jesus Will Fill You with the Holy Spirit So You Can Witness . 50
  20. Living Water 52
  21. The Most Important Thing in the Church Today 54
  22. Our Generous God 56
  23. The Power of the Promise 58

24. Prayer That Brings Down the Spirit 60
25. The Promise Fulfilled 62
26. The Promise of Pentecost 64
27. The Promise of the Holy Spirit 66
28. The Purpose of Pentecost 68
29. Receive the Holy Spirit 70
30. Receiving the Fullness of the Spirit 72
31. The Spirit on All Flesh 74
32. Springs and Streams of Living Water 76
33. Suddenly From Heaven 78
34. Times of Refreshing from the Presence of the Lord 80
35. The Two Fillings of Pentecost 82
36. What Does It Mean To Be Filled With The Holy Spirit? ... 84
37. You Can Experience the True Baptism in the Holy Spirit 86

SECTION 2 – SPIRIT-EMPOWERED MISSIONS AND MINISTRY 89

38. Advancing the Kingdom of God 90
39. All the Lord's People Prophets 92
40. The Anointing That Breaks The Yoke 94
41. Competent Ministers of the Spirit 96
42. Dunamis–Martus 98
43. Empowered for the Last Days 100
44. The Empowering of the Spirit and the Great Commission ... 102
45. God Has Chosen the Weak 104
46. The God of Every Situation 106
47. The Great Commission and the Baptism in the Holy Spirit .. 108
48. Greater Works than These 110
49. The Holy Spirit and Soul Winning 112
50. The Holy Spirit and the Ministry of the Church 114
51. Jesus' Blueprint for Building a Pentecostal Church 116

52. Jesus' Not-So-Famous Last Words 118
53. Lessons Learned from Acts 2 120
54. Men Preaching Everywhere 122
55. The Missionary Purpose of Pentecost 124
56. Mobilizing Spirit-Empowered Churches 126
57. Not By Might, Nor Power, But By My Spirit 128
58. Pentecost and World Evangelism 130
59. The Power of Pentecost 132
60. Power with Purpose 134
61. The Spirit's Desire for the Nations 136
62. We Must Never Forget 138
63. What I Have I Give to You 140
64. Witnessing in the Spirit 142
65. We Must Maintain a Missional Mindset 144
66. Why the Spirit Came 146
67. Your Daughters Shall Prophesy 148

SECTION 3 – LIFE IN THE SPIRIT 151

68. Eight Reasons You Should Be Praying In Tongues 152
69. The Fire, the Wind, and the Dove 154
70. Getting to Know Our Leader 156
71. The Gift of Tongues 158
72. The Helper 160
73. In Step with the Spirit 162
74. Life in the Spirit 164
75. Living by the Nudge 166
76. Now That You Have Been Filled with the Spirit 168
77. Obeying the Spirit's Voice 170
78. Results of Authentic Pentecostalism 172
79. Speaking in Tongues and the Baptism in the Holy Spirit 174
80. What It Means To Speak In Tongues 176

SECTION 4 – IMPORTANCE OF PENTECOST ... 179

- 81. The Acts 1:8 Church ... 180
- 82. Christ's Priority for the Church ... 182
- 83. Don't Throw Out the Baby With the Bath Water ... 184
- 84. God's Answer Comes By Fire ... 186
- 85. It's A Supernatural World ... 188
- 86. Needed: Spirit-Empowered People ... 190
- 87. Passion and Power: The Spirit's Gift to the Church ... 192
- 88. The Primacy of Pentecost ... 194
- 89. Why Receive the Holy Spirit? ... 196
- 90. Strengthening Our Pentecostal Heritage ... 198

SECTION 5 – CONFERENCE LESSONS ... 201

- 91. The Holy Spirit and the Mission of God ... 202
- 92. Spirit Baptism Revisited ... 204
- 93. What it Means to Be Pentecostal ... 206
- 94. Pentecost and the Next Generation ... 208
- 95. Women and Pentecostal Revival ... 210
- 96. The Pentecostal Bible School ... 212
- 97. How to Preach on the Baptism in the Spirit ... 214
- 98. Praying With Believers to Receive the Spirit ... 216
- 99. Planting Spirit-Empowered Missionary Churches ... 218
- 100. Leading a Local Church Into Pentecostal Revival ... 220

Sermon Text Index ... 222

Sermon Author Index

BN — Rev. Brett Nelson, USA Assemblies of God World Missions missionary, Africa. *(Sermon 77)*

CO — Rev. Dr Charles O. Osueke, General Superintendent, Assemblies of God, Nigeria, 1988-2010. *(Sermon 50)*

DC — Doug Clay, General Treasurer, Assemblies of God, USA. *(Sermon 36)*

DG — Dean Galyen, USA Assemblies of God World Missions missionary, Africa. *(Sermon 51)*

DJ — Darius Johnston, Senior Pastor, Christ Church Assembly of God, Ft. Worth Texas, USA. *(Sermon 70)*

DM — David Mensah, General Superintendent, Benin Assemblies of God. *(Sermon 25)*

DN — Don Nordin, Senior pastor, Christian Temple Assembly of God, Houston, Texas; Assistant District Superintendent, South Texas District, Assemblies of God, USA. *(Sermons 78, 89)*

DRM — Denzil R. Miller, Director, Acts in Africa Initiative; Assemblies of God World Missions missionary, Africa. *(Sermons 1, 2, 4-7, 16, 18, 21, 24, 29, 30, 32-35, 39, 41, 43-45, 47, 52-55, 60, 62-64, 67, 68, 73, 76, 88, 91, 93, 97-99)*

DT — Don Tucker, Director, Africa AG Care; Assemblies of God World Missions missionary, Africa. *(Sermon 42)*

DWC — D. Wendell Cover, Senior Pastor, Word of Life International Church, Assembly of God, Springfield, Virginia, USA. *(Sermon 79)*

DWM — Dennis W. Marquardt, District Superintendent, Northern New England District, Assemblies of God, USA. *(Sermon 15)*

EC — Edward Chitsonga, General Secretary, Malawi Assemblies of God; Senior pastor, Glorious Temple Assemblies of God Church, Lilongwe, Malawi. *(Sermon 49)*

EJ — Elwyn Johnston, Senior Pastor, Bethel Assembly of God, Temple, Texas, USA. *(Sermon 72)*

EL	Enson Lwesya, Director, All Nations Theological Seminary, Malawi; Director AAGA World Missions Commission; Team Member, Acts in Africa Initiative. *(Sermons 22, 46)*
FK	Fredrick Kyereko, Principle, Southern Ghana Bible College, Assemblies of God. *(Sermon 80)*
GRC	G. Raymond Carlson, General Superintendent, Assemblies of God, USA, 1986-1993. *(Sermon 59)*
GW	George O. Wood, General Superintendent, Assemblies of God, USA. *(Sermon 71)*
JE	John Easter, Executive Vice President, Pan-Africa Theological Seminary; Team Member, Acts in Africa Initiative; Assemblies of God World Missions missionary, Africa. *(Sermons 61, 87, 96)*
JI	John Ikoni, General Secretary, Assemblies of God, Nigeria; President, Pan-Africa Theological Seminary, Lome, Togo. *(Sermons 3, 26, 40, 90)*
JK	Jimmy Kuoh, General Superintendent, Assemblies of God, Liberia. *(Sermon 81)*
JL	John Lindell, Senior Pastor, James River Assembly of God, Springfield, MO, USA. *(Sermon 10)*
JWL	Jimmie W. Lemons, Team Member, Acts in Africa Initiative; Assemblies of God World Missions missionary, Cameroon, Africa. *(Sermons 17, 37)*
JP	Jeff Peterson, Senior Pastor, Central Assembly of God, Springfield, MO, USA. *(Sermons 83, 85)*
KB	Ken Benintendi, Assemblies of God World Missions missionary, Asia Pacific. *(Sermons 8, 9)*
KK	Ken Krucker, Director, Africa Financial Empowerment; Team Member, Acts in Africa Initiative; Assemblies of God World Missions missionary, Africa. *(Sermons 14, 23)*
LB	Leroy Bartel, Dean, College of Bible and Church Ministries, Southwestern Assemblies of God University. *(Sermon 75)*

LC	Lazarus Chakwera, General Superintendent, Malawi Assemblies of God; Chairman, Africa Assemblies of God Alliance. *(Sermons 56, 65)*
MH	Melvin Hodges, AGWM USA Latin America Regional Director, 1954-1973. *(Sermons 31, 58, 66)*
MS	Mel Surface, Chairman, Division of Adult Ministries, North Texas District Assemblies of God. *(Sermon 27)*
MT	Mark Turney, Associate Director, Acts in Africa Initiative; Assemblies of God World Missions missionary, Africa. *(Sermons 11, 12, 13, 19, 20, 38, 48, 57, 82, 86, 92, 94, 100)*
NB	Lindsay Blackburn, General Superintendent, Mauritius Assemblies of God. *(Sermon 69)*
NO	Neubueze O. Oti., Assemblies of God, Nigeria, pastor. *(Sermons 3, 26)*
SE	Scott Ennis, Assemblies of God World Missions missionary, Africa. *(Sermon 74)*
SM	Sandy Miller, Acts in Africa Initiative; Assemblies of God World Missions missionary, Africa. *(Sermon 95)*
SOA	Sebastian Obiang Abeso, General Superintendent, Assemblies of God, Equatorial Guinea. *(Sermon 84)*
WC	William Caldwell, Pentecostal Revivalist. *(Sermon 28)*

Foreword

During the last decade of the twentieth century the Africa Assemblies of God participated in a continent-wide "Decade of Harvest" emphasis. During that momentous decade, and the one following, the movement experienced great blessing and growth. The number of constituents in our churches grew from about 2 million to more than 16 million people. The number of local congregations grew from about 12,000 to about 65,000 churches. We are indeed indebted to God for His gracious blessings on our movement. Nevertheless, we as a movement of filial Assemblies of God churches in Africa choose not to dwell on the past. We rather choose to look with expectation to the present—and to the future.

Thus, on March 3-6, 2009, the General Assembly of the Africa Assemblies of God Alliance (AAGA) unanimously passed a resolution committing itself and each of its constituent national churches to another, even more aggressive, missionary emphasis. We are calling this emphasis the "Decade of Pentecost" (2010-2020). This Decade of Pentecost promises to be the most exciting and fruitful decade in the movement's almost one-hundred-year history in Africa.

In response to this initiative, Assemblies of God churches across the continent are mobilizing for aggressive evangelism, church planting, and missions thrusts. AAGA has set as its goal to see 10 million new believers baptized in the Holy Spirit and mobilized as Spirit-empowered witnesses, church planters, and missionaries during the decade. Other goals include,

- Mobilizing 100,000 intercessors to pray daily for a Pentecostal outpouring on our churches.
- Planting tens of thousands of new churches across Africa and the Indian Ocean Basin.
- Deploying hundreds of Spirit-empowered African missionaries.

- Engaging the more than 900+ yet-to-be-reached people groups in Africa.

For these things to happen we must have a genuine Pentecostal outpouring on our churches, one that focuses on being empowered by the Spirit in order to fulfill the *missio Dei* and complete the Great Commission of Christ. Therefore, we must boldly proclaim the Pentecostal message and enthusiastically lead our people into the baptism in the Holy Spirit. And we must do this at every opportunity. Only then will we be ready to engage the nations with the gospel.

In addition, during the Decade of Pentecost, the leadership of AAGA is asking every one of our pastors across Africa each Day of Pentecost to preach a missionary message focusing on the baptism in the Holy Spirit. (The Day of Pentecost occurs annually on the seventh Sunday after Easter.) We are also asking them to call their people to the front of the church and pray with them to be empowered by the Spirit to share the gospel with the lost. This book can serve as a great resource for this and similar Holy Spirit emphasis services.

I, therefore, heartily commend to you this new Decade of Pentecost publication, *Proclaiming Pentecost: 100 Sermon Outlines on the Power of the Holy Spirit*. It has been produced to aid pastors, teachers, evangelists, missionaries, and lay preachers across Africa, and around the world, to preach and teach more effectively the message of the Spirit's power. I trust that you will use this book often, and that you will preach often on the subject and pray with believers to receive the Spirit.

—Lazarus Chakwera
Chairman
Africa Assemblies of God Alliance

Introduction

The amazing growth of the Assemblies of God in Africa during the last twenty years from approximately 2 million to more than 16 million people is a powerful testimony that God is at work across this continent. Yet, while we rejoice in this great growth, we believe that this is only the beginning of what God desires to do in and through the African church.

It is undoubtedly God's will that the church in Africa be a powerful missionary church. However, for that to happen the African church must be empowered by the Holy Spirit just as the early church was (Acts 1:8). Such a church will not only be empowered to reach the hundreds of unreached tribes and the millions of unsaved people across the continent, it will also be empowered to go to *all* nations with the life-changing gospel of Christ.

This collection of sermon outlines on the power of the Holy Spirit has been compiled to assist men and women who have a passion to see the church of Africa become a Holy Spirit-empowered missionary church. If the African church is to fulfill God's mission, it is imperative that pastors, church leaders and other committed disciples preach and teach regularly on the baptism in the Holy Spirit and give their listeners the opportunity to receive the Spirit. If we will be faithful to proclaim the message of Pentecost, God will be faithful to fulfill his promise of "power from on high".

These sermons come from a select group of Pentecostal ministers and missionaries from Africa and the USA who are passionate about the great need for the African church to experience the power of Pentecost. While the predominant theme of each message is the power of the Holy Spirit, you will discover that the messages are also missional in focus. It is true that the presence and power of the Holy Spirit brings great personal blessing into our lives, however we must never lose sight of the fact that this gift was given for a purpose. We seek the Spirit's power to enable us to accomplish God's mission.

How to Use this Book

Each of the one hundred sermon outlines in this book has been edited to fit onto a maximum of two pages. In doing this we have attempted to include enough content in each outline to give the reader a clear indication of the structure and flow of the message. At the same time, we have sought to be brief enough to give preachers and teachers ample room to develop and customize the messages to the unique needs of their listeners. As you study, pray over and preach these outlines, we trust that the Holy Spirit will inspire you with fresh ideas of how to develop your own messages on the power of the Holy Spirit and God's Mission.

If we are to effectively preach on the baptism in the Holy Spirit we must spend much time in study and prayer, allowing the Spirit to fill our hearts with the message. We are confident that the Spirit will help you to preach these messages better than they have ever been preached before –and with greater results. As you study and prepare to preach on the power of the Holy Spirit, we urge you to spend much time in prayer asking God to powerfully fill you with His Spirit to enable you to proclaim His word.

This book is divided into five sections. The first four sections are thematic in content, while the final section contains messages as they are presented in Acts 1:8 conferences conducted by the Acts in Africa team around the continent. You may want to use this final section to conduct your own Acts 1:8 conference to mobilize your church or group of churches in Spirit-empowered missions.

Contributors

At the end of each outline you will find the initials of the author of that sermon in brackets. If you so desire, you can find out more about the author in the Author Index on page seven. Finally, I wish to thank each of the 36 contributors for helping to ensure that the message of Pentecost will continue to be proclaimed throughout Africa and beyond until Jesus comes again.

Mark R. Turney
Associate Director
Acts in Africa Initiative

Section 1

The Baptism in the Holy Spirit

The Acts 1:8 Promise of Jesus

Sermon in a Sentence: Jesus promised to empower every one of His followers to be His witnesses.

Sermon Purpose: To see believers baptized in the Holy Spirit and empowered as Christ's witnesses.

Text: Acts 1:4-8

Introduction
1. It is God's will for every believer in this place to be baptized in the Holy Spirit and empowered for the task of evangelism and missions.
2. Jesus' promise in Acts 1:8 is His last and most important promise to the church.
   a. He first fulfilled this promise on the Day of Pentecost.
   b. Pentecost launched a powerful first-century missionary movement.
   c. Luke describes it like this: (Read Ac 2:1-4).
3. But what did it all mean?
   a. It meant that Jesus had begun to fulfill His Acts 1:8 Promise.
   b. Supernatural power entered into these disciples.
   c. They were changed on the inside.
   d. They became powerful Spirit-anointed witnesses.
4. Our prayer is that Jesus will fulfill His Acts 1:8 Promise in our midst today.
5. From this promise of Jesus we learn four powerful truths:

I. WE LEARN ABOUT JESUS' PROMISE OF POWER.
("But you will receive power...")
   A. Jesus has given us an important task.
      1. That is, to be His witnesses beginning at home and continuing to the whole world.
      2. Humanly speaking, It is an impossible task.
      3. Think how those first disciples must have felt.
   B. And yet, Jesus promised power to accomplish the task.
      1. It would be supernatural power.
      2. It is a promise to every believer.
   C. Question: Who is the "you" Jesus mentions in Acts 1:8?
      1. First, it refers to His apostles.
         a. They had been saved, called, and commissioned.
         b. We are much like them. We, too, have been saved, called, and commissioned.
      2. "You" also includes all believers everywhere (Ac 2:38-39).

3. "You" also includes every person here today.
4. It includes you! (Ac 2:39).

II. WE LEARN ABOUT THE SOURCE OF THAT POWER.
("... when the Holy Spirit comes upon you")
A. The source of power is the Holy Spirit.
B. The Holy Spirit provides supernatural enablement:
   1. To be Christ's witness.
   2. To preach and teach with power.
   3. To do the works of Jesus.
   4. To advance the kingdom of God.

III. WE LEARN ABOUT THE PURPOSE OF THE POWER.
("... and you will be My witnesses in Jerusalem, and in all Judea and Samaria, and to the ends of the earth.")
A. The Spirit gives us power to obey Christ's command to preach the gospel in both our home and to the ends of the earth.
B. Unfortunately, too many Pentecostals have missed this truth.
C. We must all participate in proclaiming the gospel.

IV. WE LEARN SOMETHING ABOUT WHEN AND HOW WE RECEIVE THAT POWER.
("...when the Holy Spirit comes upon you")
A. This power to witness does not come automatically at conversion or water baptism.
   1. There is something we must do to receive this power.
   2. To receive the power we must, by faith, receive the Holy Spirit (Gal 3:2, 14).
B. Jesus taught us how to receive: (Read: Lk 11:9-13)
   1. First, you must ask in faith (Lk 11:9, 13).
   2. Next, you must receive by faith (Lk 11:10; Mk 11:24).
   3. Then, you must speak in faith (Ac 2:4; Jn 7:38)

Conclusion and Altar Call
Come now and receive Jesus' Acts 1:8 Promise.

[DRM]

2 The Baptism in the Holy Spirit

Sermon in a Sentence: You can be baptized in the Holy Spirit today.
Purpose: To see believers baptized in the Holy Spirit
Text: Acts 1:8; 2:1-4

Introduction
1. There is nothing more important in the Christian's life than being baptized in the Spirit.
2. In this message we will answer three questions about the baptism in the Holy Spirit.

I. WHAT IS THE BAPTISM IN THE HOLY SPIRIT?
A. It is a powerful, life-changing experience from God by which God clothes and fills a believer with His power and presence (Lk 24:49; Ac 1:8; Ac 2:1-4).
B. It is a promise for all believers (Ac 2:4; Ac 2:14-17; Ac 2:38-39).
C. It a command to all believers (Ac 1:4-5; Eph 5:18).

II. WHY IS THE BAPTISM IN THE HOLY SPIRIT SO IMPORTANT IN EVERY BELIEVER'S LIFE?
A. Because it is the Christian's source of power for life and service (Ac 1:8; Ac 4:31-33).
B. Because, when you are baptized in the Holy Spirit, you will receive power to witness (Ac 1:8).
C. Because, when you are baptized in the Spirit, you will also receive power to do the following:
   1. Power to overcome temptation and live a holy life (Ro 1:4; 8:13).
   2. Power to pray more effectively (Lk 11:1-13; Ro 8:26-28).
   3. Power to love more ardently (Ro 5:5).
   4. Power to better understand the Word of God (1Co 2:14; Jn 14:26; 16:13).
   5. Power to preach more effectively (Ac 4:8, 31; 1Co 2:4).
   6. Power to do the works of Jesus (Jn 14:12 with Jn 14:16; 16:7).
   7. Power to more clearly discern the voice of God (Ro 8:16).
   8. Power to worship (Jn 4:24).

III. HOW CAN YOU BE FILLED WITH THE HOLY SPIRIT TODAY?

A. Three things you must do *before* you can be filled with the Spirit.
   1. You must be truly born again (Ac 2:38; Jn 14:17).
   2. You must hunger and thirst after God (Mt 5:6; Jn 7:37).
   3. You must be prepared to obey God and become His witness (Ac 5:32).
B. You receive the Spirit through faith.
   1. Faith is the essential ingredient for receiving anything from God (Gal 3:2, 5, 14).
   2. You must believe God for the Spirit (Jn 7:38).
C. Take these three steps of faith:
   1. Ask in faith (Lk 11:9, 13).
   2. Receive by faith (Lk 11:10; Mk 11:24).
   3. In faith, speak out of your innermost being (Ac 2:4; Jn 7:37).

Conclusion and Altar Call

Come now to be baptized in the Holy Spirit.

[DRM]

The Baptism in the Holy Spirit Is What We Need

Sermon in a Sentence: If we are going to have power to resist and change our environments, we must each be baptized in the Holy Spirit.

Sermon Purpose: That believers understand their need to be empowered by in the Holy Spirit and that they seek and receive the baptism in the Holy Spirit.

Texts: Luke 24:49; Acts 1:4-8; 8:14-17; 19:1-7

Introduction
1. Receiving the baptism in the Holy Spirit is the solution to the lukewarmness, worldliness, and shallow faith in the church and in our own lives today.
2. The worship atmosphere in the church today reveals a church in dire need of the power of the Holy Spirit.

I. A SICK CHURCH
A. When Paul arrived in Ephesus he found a sick church.
   1. It was small and weak.
   2. It was unable to impact its city for Christ.
B. The church was being oppressed and suffocated by its environment.
   1. Worship of the goddess Diana dominated the city.
   2. Worship of Diana involved witchcraft, black magic, sorcery, and sexual perversion.
   3. The church was powerless to combat these demonic forces.
C. Many churches today are in the same condition.
   1. They are being suffocated by their environments
   2. They are carnal, weak, and powerless to combat the evils of their environments.

II. PRESCRIPTION FOR THE CURE
A. Paul knew the cure for the church's sickness—the baptism in the Holy Spirit.
B. The church in Ephesus needed two remedies:
   1. *Knowledge:* They needed their theology straightened out.
   2. *Experience:* They needed the power of the Spirit.
   3. Paul addressed both issues:
      a. He straightened out their knowledge (Ac 19:1-4).
      b. He led them into experience (Ac 19:5-6).
C. The same is true of the church today.

1. We must understand what the Bible teaches about the baptism in the Holy Spirit:
   a. It is separate from salvation.
   b. It is for all believers.
   c. It is for power to witness and represent Christ.
   d. It is evidenced by speaking in tongues.
2. Like the twelve Ephesian disciples we must each experience the baptism in the Holy Spirit.

III. BENEFITS OF THE HOLY SPIRIT BAPTISM
A. Many benefits come from receiving the Spirit, including:
   1. The personal presence of Jesus is made more real (Jn 14:15-17; 16:14-15).
   2. We are enabled to live holy lives (Ro 8:2, 13).
   3. We are helped with our prayers (Ro 8:26-27).
   4. We are comforted in times of trouble (Jn 14:16, 26; 15:26; 16:7 [KJV]; Ac 18:9-11).
B. The most important benefit is that we receive power to be Christ's witnesses (Ac 1:8).

IV. RECEIVE THE HOLY SPIRIT
A. We receive the Spirit as individuals (Ac 9:17-18).
B. We must be earnestly hunger for the experience (Mt 5:6; Jn 7:37).
C. We must repent and ask for the Holy Spirit (Ac 2:38).
D. We must have faith (Jn 7:38; Mk 11:24).

Conclusion and Altar Call
1. Only as believers are filled with the Spirit will the church be powerful enough to resist the effects of its environment.
2. Only then will we have power to impact and change our cities and villages for Christ.
3. Come now to be filled with the Spirit.

[JI and NO]

Adapted from "Lesson 3: The Need for the Baptism in the Holy Spirit" in *The Relevance of the Holy Spirit in Today's Church* by Rev. Dr. John O. Ikoni and Rev. Neubueze O. Oti. (Aba, Nigeria: Assemblies of God Press, 2009).

Baptism in the Holy Spirit Series
No. 1 of 4
What is the Baptism in the Holy Spirit?

Sermon in a Sentence: The baptism in the Holy Spirit is a powerful spiritual experience for all believers in Christ.
Sermon Purpose: That every believer will come to desire and receive the baptism in the Holy Spirit
Text: Luke 3:16

Introduction
1. In our text John the Baptist spoke of an experience for Christ's followers called the baptism in the Holy Spirit.
2. In this message we will answer the important question, "What is the baptism in the Holy Spirit?"

I. THE BAPTISM IN THE HOLY SPIRIT IS A WONDERFUL PROMISE FROM GOD.
  A. Jesus called the baptism in the Holy Spirit "*the* Promise of the Father" (Lk 24:49; Ac 1:4).
  B. Jesus gave wonderful promises concerning the gift of the Holy Spirit (see Lk 11:9-13).
  C. The disciples received the promise of the Spirit on the Day of Pentecost (Ac 2:4, 33).

II. THE BAPTISM IN THE HOLY SPIRIT IS A POWERFUL, PRESENT-DAY, LIFE-CHANGING EXPERIENCE.
  A. It is a powerful experience.
   1. It is described in terms of power (Lk 24:49; Ac 1:8).
   2. It results in powerful ministry (Ac 4:33).
  B. It is a present-day experience.
   1. It is for all generations of Christians (Ac 2:39).
   2. It occurred again and again in Acts (2:4; 8:17-18; 9:18-10; 10:44-46; 19:6).
  C. It is a life-changing experience.
   1. It changed the disciples from cowards to powerful witnesses.
   2. It will change you too!

III. THE BAPTISM IN THE HOLY SPIRIT IS AN INVASION FROM HEAVEN.
  A. At Pentecost a sound "from heaven" was heard.
   1. The experience comes from heaven (that is, from God).
   2. They were "clothed with power from on high" (that is, from God).

    B. The Spirit comes as a "holy invasion" from heaven.
       1. Examples in Acts: 1:8; 4:31; 10:44
       2. You can expect the Holy Spirit to come on you like an invasion from heaven.

IV. THE BAPTISM IN THE HOLY SPIRIT IS ALSO A PERMEATION WITHIN (That is, a Complete Filling of Every Part of One's Being).

    A. The term "filled with the Holy Spirit" is often used to describe the experience.
       1. It is used six times in Acts.
       2. It is used for the first time in Acts 2:4.
    B. Spirit baptism is not only to be thought of as a holy invasion from the outside, but also as a radical transformation occurring on the inside.
       1. Illustration: Like a sponge is filled with water.
    C. To receive the Spirit's fullness we must open our lives completely to God.

V. THE BAPTISM IN THE HOLY SPIRIT IS A BIBLICAL COMMAND.

    A. The experience is so essential to the Christian life that the Bible does not present it to us as an option.
    B. Both Jesus and Paul command us to be filled (Ac 1:4-5; Eph 5:18).
    C. How blessed we are when we obey!

VI. THE BAPTISM IN THE HOLY SPIRIT IS AN EXPERIENCE FOR ALL BELIEVERS.

    A. Note how often the word "all" is used in speaking of the baptism in the Holy Spirit in the Bible (Num 11:29; Joel 2:28; Ac 2:4; Ac 4:31)
    B. In Luke 11, Jesus changes the terminology from "all" to "everyone" (Lk 11:10; ref. Ac 2:39).

Conclusion and Altar Call
    1. Are you ready to let the Spirit transform your life?
    2. Come and be filled with the Spirit today.

[DRM]

Baptism in the Holy Spirit Series
No. 2 of 4
Why is the Baptism in the Holy Spirit a Necessity for Every Believer?

Sermon in a Sentence: It is essential that every believer be baptized in the Holy Spirit.
Sermon's Purpose: To encourage and see believers be baptized in the Holy Spirit
Texts: Acts 1:4-5, Ephesians 5:18

Introduction
1. Our texts contain two commands to believers to be filled with the Holy Spirit, one from Jesus and one from Paul.
2. These commands demonstrate the necessity of one's being baptized in the Holy Spirit.
3. We will discuss why we must each be filled with the Spirit today.

I. **WE MUST EACH BE FILLED WITH THE SPIRIT BECAUSE WE HAVE A LIFE TO LIVE THAT IS BEYOND OUR ABILITY.**
   A. Look at the life God calls on us to live:
      1. A life like Jesus lived (1Jn 2:6).
      2. A life of purity (1Pe 1:15-16).
      3. A life of love (Mt 5:43-44).
   B. But we are weak and unable in our own strength to live such a life.
      1. We are more apt to hate, envy, and complain.
      2. We are more apt to live like the world than to live like Jesus.
      3. We cry out like Paul, "O wretched man that I am, who shall deliver me . . .?" (Ro 7:24).
      4. The answer comes back, "Don't despair, we have help from above!" (ref. Gal 5:16)
   C. An important question: How do we get this help from God?
      1. We begin by hungering and thirsting for more of God (Mt 5:6).
      2. In Matthew 5:6, note our part and God's part:
         a. Our part, "hunger and thirst after . . ."
         b. God's part, "they shall be filled . . ."

II. **WE MUST EACH BE FILLED WITH THE SPIRIT BECAUSE WE HAVE A JOB TO DO THAT IS GREATER THAN OUR RESOURCES.**
   A. Jesus left us with a big job.
      1. It is called the Great Commission.

  2. Mt 28:19-20
  3. Mt 24:14
 B. But our own resources are inadequate for the job.
  1. Our personal resources are inadequate.
  2. Our financial resources are inadequate.
 C. And yet, Jesus has promised us power to get the job done:
  1. In Acts 1 He gave His disciples a promise and a command:
   a. *The promise* (1:8): "You will be my witnesses. . . to the end of the earth."
   b. *The command* (1:4-5): "Do not leave Jerusalem, but wait for the gift my Father promised . . ."
  2. We cannot fulfill the promise until we first obey the command.

Conclusion and Altar Call
 1. You have a life to live that is beyond your ability.
 2. You have a job to do that is beyond your resources.
 3. You need to receive God's power.
 4. Come and be filled with the Spirit today.

                 [DRM]

Baptism in the Holy Spirit Series
No. 3 of 4
How to Receive the Baptism in the Holy Spirit

Sermon in a Sentence: Let the Holy Spirit fill and change your life today.
Sermon Purpose: That believers will be filled and/or refilled with the Holy Spirit
Text: Luke 11:9-13

Introduction
1. In this passage Jesus instructs His disciples on how to receive the gift of the Holy Spirit.
2. In this message we will discuss how you can receive the Holy Spirit today.

I. THE CONTEXT IN WHICH THE HOLY SPIRIT IS RECEIVED
A. The Spirit is received in the context of prayer.
   1. In our text Jesus was answering the disciples' question, "Lord teach us to pray" (v. 1).
   2. Jesus was praying when he was anointed by the Spirit (Lk 3:21-22).
   3. Paul was praying when he was filled (Ac 9:11-12, 17).
   4. Prayer is key.
B. The Spirit is received in the context of obedience to preach the gospel (Ac 5:32).
C. The Spirit is received in the context of humility (1Pe 5:6).
D. The Spirit is received in the context of faith (Gal 3:2, 5, 14).
   1. Jesus: "*Whoever believes* in me, as the Scripture has said, streams of living water will flow from within him" (Jn 7:38).

II. TO RECEIVE THE HOLY SPIRIT, DO THIS:
A. Approach the throne of grace with boldness knowing that you are in the perfect will of God (Heb 4:16; 1Jn 5:14-15).
B. Ask in bold faith.
   1. Claim His promises (Lk 11:9-13).
   2. Expect God to fill you (Mk 11:24).
   3. Expect to speak in tongues (Ac 2:4).
   4. Prepare to be Christ's witness (Ac 1:8).
C. Receive the Spirit by an act of faith.
   1. The Spirit is not received passively.
   2. ILLUS: Much like Peter stepping out of the boat to walk on the water, we must step out in faith believing God to fill us (ref. Mt 14:25-29).

- D. Sense the Spirit's presence within.
    1. Focus your attention on God and what He is doing in your heart.
    2. Sense His presence upon you and within you.
- E. Speak in faith (Ac 2:4).
    1. Allow this power and presence to flow out (Jn 7:37-38).
    2. Speak as the Spirit gives you the words.

Conclusion and Altar Call
Come now to be filled with the Spirit

[DRM]

Baptism in the Holy Spirit Series
No. 4 of 4
Our Responsibility Concerning the Baptism in the Holy Spirit

Sermon in a Sentence: Once you have been baptized in the Holy Spirit you have certain responsibilities to fulfill.

Sermon Purpose: To inspire people to be baptized in the Spirit and to encourage those who have been baptized in the Spirit to begin to minister in the Spirit

Text: 2 Corinthians 3:7-10: (note the phrase "ministry of the Spirit")

Introduction
1. In our text Paul compares two kinds of ministry:
    a. i.e., Ministry under the Law and the ministry in the Spirit.
    b. One brings death, the other brings righteousness.
    c. One is glorious, the other is more glorious.
2. New Testament ministry is thus described as "ministry of the Spirit."
    a. Ministry of the Spirit is ministry "which is empowered by the Spirit and results in others receiving the Spirit" (Gordon D. Fee).
    b. This message will focus on our responsibility in leading others into the baptism in the Holy Spirit.
3. The Bible teaches five responsibilities of believers in regard to the baptism in the Holy Spirit:

I. WE MUST PERSONALLY EXPERIENCE IT.
   A. We have all been commanded to be filled with the Spirit (Ac 1:4-5; Eph 5:18).
      1. Jesus was filled with the Spirit (Lk 3:26; Ac 10:38).
      2. The disciples were filled with the Spirit (Ac 2:4; 4:31, 33).
   B. Have you experienced the baptism in the Holy Spirit?

II. WE MUST DAILY WALK IN IT.
   A. The Bible commands us to "walk in the Spirit."
      1. Ro 8:1 (KJV); Gal 5:16, 25.
      2. Gal 3:3.
   B. We must "stir up" the gift of the Spirit inside us (2Ti 1:6).
   C. Christian leader, your people's greatest need is your own authentic walk in the Spirit.

III. WE MUST FAITHFULLY PROCLAIM AND TEACH IT.
   A. Jesus taught and proclaimed the message of the baptism in the Holy Spirit (Lk 11:9-13; Jn 14–16; Ac 1:4-8).
   B. Peter preached about the baptism in the Spirit:

       1. In his first sermon at Pentecost (Ac 2:14-17; 38-39).
       2. In his second sermon (Ac 3:19).
  C. Paul preached and taught about the baptism in the Holy Spirit.
       1. In Ephesus (Ac 19:1-7).
       2. In his epistles (for instance, Eph 5:18)
  D. Have you been preaching about the baptism in the Holy Spirit? Will you?

IV. WE MUST KNOW HOW TO LEAD OTHERS INTO THE EXPERIENCE.
  A. This is a primary responsibility of every Pentecostal pastor.
  B. Jesus and the apostles were serious about leading others into the experience:
       1. Jesus before He returned to heaven (Lk 24:45-49).
       2. The apostles in Samaria (Ac 8:15-17).
       3. Paul in Ephesus (Ac 19:1-7).
  C. We must imitate Jesus and the apostles.

V. WE MUST PROVIDE OPPORTUNITIES FOR OUR PEOPLE TO EXPERIENCE IT.
  A. We must create the right atmosphere in the church.
  B. We must preach often on the subject.
  C. We must pray with believers to receive.
  D. We must teach others how to pray with others.

Conclusion and Altar Call
1. Don't neglect this precious gift.
2. Come now to be filled and re-filled with the Spirit.

[DRM]

The Comforter Has Come

Sermon in a Sentence: Jesus promised the presence and power of the Spirit to enable all of us to live and witness for Him.
Sermon Purpose: To see people filled with the Spirit and witness
Text: John 14:12-20; 16:7; Acts 1:8

Introduction
1. Christianity is rooted in four great events.
    a. Christmas: the personal entrance of God through His Son into human life.
    b. Good Friday: Christ's work of revelation, reconciliation and redemption.
    c. Easter: the victory of God through Jesus Christ over the powers of sin and death
    d. Pentecost: the empowering of God's people with the same power which was in Christ through the Holy Spirit.
2. Pentecost speaks to us of the "coming of the Holy Spirit upon the church"
    a. The Comforter has come!

I. LET US CONSIDER THE PROMISE OF THE SPIRIT.
   A. On several occasions Jesus spoke about this promise.
      1. Jesus promised that everyone who believed in Him would receive the Spirit like a river of living water in his or her life (Jn 7:37-39).
      2. Jesus told the disciples He would soon be leaving them, but He would send the Holy Spirit, to take His place (Jn 14:16-17 and 16:7).
      3. Before ascending to heaven, He told the disciples to wait until they received the promise of the Spirit (Ac 1:4-5).
   B. At Pentecost Jesus first fulfilled the promise (Ac 2:1-4).
   C. Then, under the anointing of the Spirit, Peter declared to the crowd that the promise of the Spirit was for all (Ac 2:38-39).
      1. Thus, the promise of "forgiveness of sins" and "the gift of the Holy Spirit" was not just for them, it reaches to us today.

II. LET US CONSIDER THE PRESENCE OF THE SPIRIT.
   A. First, Jesus promised that the Comforter would be with us forever (John 14:16,18).
      1. He will not leave us as orphans (v. 18).
      2. Jesus was saying to the disciples, "I am not abandoning you. I have a long term plan. I am leaving, so the Holy Spirit can come.

       3. He was also saying that this is not a step backwards (Jn 16:7).
          a. This is part of my master plan to spread the gospel to the ends of the earth.
          b. He wanted them to realize that it was best for Him to leave.
          c. If He stayed on earth
              1) the ministry would be localized.
              2) it would be impossible for Him to communicate with his disciples equally at all times and in all places.
   B. Second, Jesus promised that the Holy Spirit would not only be *with* us but *in* us (John 14:17).
       1. What an amazing promise: God will come to live inside of us and give us an undeniable experience of His presence
       2. It will confirm to us that Christ is in us (Jn 14:20).

III. LET US CONSIDER THE POWER OF THE SPIRIT.
   A. Jesus taught that when the Holy Spirit comes upon us, we are empowered to witness (Ac 1:8).
       1. He wanted His disciples to know that the coming of the "Counselor" would equip them for a much wider and more powerful ministry (Jn 14:12).
       2. He would fill them with so much power that their ministry would have an even wider impact than His own.
   B. The Spirit is a witnessing Spirit.
       1. When He fills us with His power, He does so in order that we may be equipped to be a powerful witness for Christ (Jn 15:26-27).
   C. Today, just like we see in the book of Acts, the power of the Spirit will guide us, give us the ability to live holy lives, and empower us to effectively share our faith with others.

Conclusion and Altar Call
Come now and receive the gift of the Holy Spirit in your life

[KB]

Common Questions About the Baptism in the Holy Spirit

Sermon in a Sentence: The Bible answers many common questions about the Baptism in the Holy Spirit.

Sermon Purpose: To help believers desire to be empowered by the Holy Spirit as Christ's witness.

Introduction
Let us consider some commonly asked questions about the baptism in the Holy Spirit:

I. **DO CHRISTIANS RECEIVE THE HOLY SPIRIT WHEN THEY ARE SAVED?**
   A. When you accepted Christ, you can be sure that the Holy Spirit was at work (Ro 8:9).
   B. Each of us who have come to Christ have experienced the gracious work of the Holy Spirit in the new birth (Jn 3:3-6).

II. **HOW THEN IS THE BAPTISM IN THE HOLY SPIRIT DIFFERENT FROM SALVATION?**
   A. There is an additional and distinct ministry of the Holy Spirit called the baptism in the Holy Spirit (Ac 1:4-5,8).
      1. This is an empowering gift from God the Father promised to every believer.
      2. Holy Spirit baptism helps us to live holy lives and gives us a deepening devotion and commitment to Jesus.
   B. The primary purpose of the baptism of the Holy Spirit, however, is to give us power and boldness to witness to others of our faith (Ac 1:8).
   C. We all need this "Empowering Gift" from God to live a victorious life and to share our faith more effectively.
      1. This experience is so important Jesus told the disciples to not leave Jerusalem until they received it (Ac 1:4-5).

III. **CAN A PERSON BE FILLED WITH THE HOLY SPIRIT WITHOUT SPEAKING IN TONGUES?**
   A. To answer this we must stay close to the biblical pattern.
      1. At Pentecost "all of them were filled with the Holy Spirit and began to speak in other tongues as the Spirit enabled them" (Acts 2:4)
      2. At the household of Cornelius "the Holy Spirit came on all who heard the message" and "they heard them speaking in tongues and praising God" (Acts 10:46).

3. In Ephesus "when Paul placed his hands on them, the Holy Spirit came on them, and they spoke in tongues and prophesied" (Acts 19:6).
   B. These passages demonstrate that the "initial physical evidence" of being baptized in the Holy Spirit is speaking in tongues.

IV. WHAT IS THE ADVANTAGE OF PRAYING IN TONGUES IN ONE'S PRIVATE PRAYER LIFE?
   A. It serves to confirm that you have received the Spirit.
   B. It will edify you in your spiritual life and in your walk with God (1Co 14:2,4; Jude 20).
   C. When we pray in tongues, the Spirit helps us pray (Ro 8:26).
      1. At times when our earthly language seems inadequate to share our hearts with God, prayer in tongues takes us beyond the limitations of intellect as the Spirit prays through us.

V. WORDS OF ENCOURAGEMENT FOR THOSE WHO HAVE NOT YET BEEN BAPTIZED IN THE HOLY SPIRIT:
   A. If these things are still unclear to you, study God's Word and seek God for understanding.
      1. Remember, God loves us all the same.
      2. The Holy Spirit comes to comfort us, to guide us into all truth, and to empower us for witness.
      3. Seek to receive the Spirit, not to just speak in tongues.
   B. Being filled with the Spirit is only a beginning.
      1. After that it is your responsibility to keep your experience fresh and alive in you each day.

Conclusion and Altar Call
   1. May our prayer always be: "Come, Holy Spirit, I need thee!"
   2. Join me in inviting the Holy Spirit into your life.
   3. May you experience your own personal Pentecost!

[KB]

10. The Day of Pentecost

Sermon in a Sentence: Understanding the Day of Pentecost leads us to believe and seek to be filled with the Spirit.

Sermon Purpose: That people will be filled with the Spirit and become effective witnesses.

Text: Acts 2:1-12

I. **THE EXPLANATION OF THE SPIRIT'S COMING** (Ac 2:1a).
   A. Pentecost in Greek means fiftieth.
      1. The Jews call it the "Feast of Weeks" (Lev 23:15-21).
      2. The Old Testament ceremonial law pictured Christ and His work (Gal 3:24; Col 2:16,17).
   B. First Picture: The Passover (Lev 23:5, 1Co 5:7).
      1. Passover reminded people of how God saved Israel out of slavery in Egypt.
      2. The Passover lamb is a picture of the work Christ did for us when He died on the cross to save us from sin.
   C. Second Picture: The Feast of First Fruits (Lev 23:9-10).
      1. Celebrated on the first day of the week after Passover.
      2. People offered part of their barley harvest to God.
      3. It was called "first fruits" because it was symbolic of the rest of the crop which would soon be harvested.
      4. It is a picture of Christ's resurrection on the first day of the week after Passover (1Co 15:20-23).
   D. Third Picture: Feast of Weeks/Pentecost (Lev 23:15-17, Acts 2:1). Note: Two things connected with this celebration:
      1. *It celebrated the coming grain harvest:*
         a. Pentecost is about harvest! (Ac 2:14, 16-17, 21).
         b. The purpose of being filled with the Spirit is so we might be empowered as witnesses for the Lord to bring about a great harvest of the lost (Ac 1:8).
      2. *It celebrated the new covenant in Christ.*
         a. God made a covenant with Abraham and promised to bless the whole world through him (Ge 12:3).
         b. God planned to use the Jewish nation to lead people to faith in the Messiah (Ex 19:5-6).
         c. The rabbis taught that 50 days after Passover, God descended on Mount Sinai and gave the covenant.
         d. However, Israel failed to keep the covenant, so God promised to make a new covenant (Jer 31:31-34).
         e. Now in Acts 2:1 we read that 50 days after Passover God again descended to enact a new covenant.

II. **THE EVIDENCE OF THE SPIRIT'S COMING** (Ac 2:1b-4).

A. The Wind (v.2).
   1. Jesus compared the Holy Spirit to wind (Jn 3:8).
   2. At Pentecost this is not described as a gentle breeze but as a powerful wind, as if it was the very breath of God.
   3. This sound caused the crowd to gather (Ac 2:6a).
B. The Fire (v.3).
   1. It wasn't actual fire, but seemed like fire.
   2. It was a visible manifestation of the Spirit's presence.
C. They were all filled with the Holy Spirit (v. 4a).
   1. The Greek word for filled, *pleroo,* describes how wind fills the sail of a ship so that it is moved by the wind.
   2. The meaning is that the disciples were yielded to the control of the Spirit, and He was moving them to act.
   3. Acts tells us that this is same thing happened repeatedly in these disciples' lives (Ac 4:8, 31).
D. They spoke in tongues as the Spirit enabled them (v. 4b).
   1. They were speaking in languages they did not know.
   2. This was a miracle that the Spirit enabled them to do.

III. THE EFFECT OF THE SPIRIT'S COMING (Ac 2:5-12).
A. The Crowd was comprised of people from many nations (vv. 5, 9-11).
B. The Confusion (vv. 6-8,12).
   1. The crowd heard uneducated people proclaiming the wonders of God in languages from around the world.
   2. They must have thought: "How was this possible? It must be a miracle! What does it mean?"
C. The Culmination (Ac 2:41).
   1. This was the work of God setting the stage for the presentation of the gospel and the work of bringing salvation and blessing to the nations.
D. This brings us to four conclusions:
   1. God's timing is perfect and His Word will be fulfilled.
   2. We too will receive His power if we will obey His will.
      a. The 120 were filled with the Spirit because they obeyed Christ (Ac 1:4,13-14; 2:1).
   3. This gift of the Spirit is for everyone (Ac 2:17, 39).
   4. God has done all of this so that we might effectively share Christ with others and lead them to salvation

Conclusion and Altar Call
Let us come and pray that God will fill us with the Spirit and empower us to be His witnesses.

[JL]

11. Did You Receive the Spirit When You Believed?

Sermon in a Sentence: The baptism in the Holy Spirit is a priority because God's purpose is to give every believer power to be a witness.

Sermon Purpose: To convince believers that they need the baptism in the Holy Spirit and help to prepare them to receive it.

Text: Acts 19:1-12

I. **THE PRIORITY OF THE BAPTISM IN THE HOLY SPIRIT**
   A. Paul's question: Did you receive the Spirit when you believed?
      1. This question implies the possibility of being a disciple and yet not being filled with the Holy Spirit.
      2. It also implies this is a priority for Christians.
      3. Paul wanted to know for sure they had been filled with the Spirit, because he was concerned that the new church in Ephesus be a truly Pentecostal church.
   B. This same priority on Spirit baptism is seen in Samaria (Ac 8:14-17).
   C. Spirit baptism is so important that it is not to be just a one time experience but a continual experience.
      1. Years later Paul wrote to the church in Ephesus and urged them to be filled with the Spirit and to remain filled with the Spirit (Eph 5:18).
      2. "Be filled with the Spirit" is, in the Greek, a command to maintain a constant state of being filled.
   D. The early church made this a priority, and we should too.

II. **THE PURPOSE OF THE BAPTISM IN THE HOLY SPIRIT: POWERFUL WITNESS.**
   A. Paul was concerned that these men be filled with the Spirit because of God's purpose for Spirit baptism.
      1. Jesus defined the purpose of Spirit baptism (Ac 1:8).
      2. Spirit baptism is not for personal benefit and blessing but for power to serve God's mission.
      3. Paul knew these 12 disciples needed power to witness.
   B. The result of these 12 men being filled with the Spirit:
      1. They were filled with the Spirit and began to speak in tongues and prophesy by the power of the Spirit (Ac 19:6).
      2. As a result, a powerful witness went forth in that whole region (Ac 19:8-10).
   C. It was Paul's plan to spread the gospel through all of Asia.

            1. Acts 19:9-10 implies that Paul was not the only one preaching and being used by God.
            2. Paul's reason for making Spirit baptism a priority in Ephesus was because he planned to reach all of Asia through the witness of Spirit-filled believers.
            3. Other Asian churches are mentioned in the New Testament that may have been started as a result of Paul's ministry in Ephesus.
            4. Paul was following the plan Christ gave the church: Be filled with the Spirit and witness (Ac 1:8).
    D. God's plan has not changed, He is still calling people to seek the power of His Spirit to be witnesses.

III. **THE PREPARATION FOR RECEIVING THE HOLY SPIRIT**
    A. Step one: Repentance from sin.
        1. The men in Ephesus had accepted John the Baptist's message to repent from sin.
    B. Step two: Faith in Christ as Lord and Savior.
        1. When Paul realized that the men in Ephesus had only heard John's message, he explained to them that John the Baptist had come to prepare people for Jesus.
        2. John the Baptist preached two things:
            a. Repent because the Kingdom of heaven is very close (Mt 3:2).
            b. There is one coming who will take away the sin of the world. (Jesus, Jn 1:29)
        3. When they understood, they accepted Christ (Ac 19:5).
    C. Step three: Believe that Christ will fill you with the Spirit.
        1. John's message included the promise that Jesus would baptize with the Holy Spirit (Lk 3:16).
    D. Step four: Ask God to fill you with the Spirit.
        1. The men believed, and when Paul placed his hands on them, they began to pray and were filled with the Spirit (Ac 19:6).
        2. You, too, can receive the Spirit, if you will ask in prayer.

Conclusion and Altar Call
    1. Like the disciples in Ephesus prepare to receive the Holy Spirit.
    2. Open your heart to God and believe that this is what God wants to do for you.
    3. Ask God to do it for you.

[MT]

12. Don't Leave Home Without It

Sermon in a Sentence: Christ's final command to His disciples was that they must receive the power of the Holy Spirit in order to accomplish the Great Commission.

Sermon Purpose: To see believers obey Christ's final command to be baptized with the Holy Spirit and receive power to be His witnesses.

Text: Acts 1:4-5, 8

Introduction
1. A person's last words are usually of primary importance to that person.
2. Jesus' last words to the church, before He ascended to heaven, are a command for every believer.
3. In this command Jesus made it clear that the baptism in the Holy Spirit must be a priority in every Christian's life.

I. **CHRIST'S FINAL COMMAND** (Ac 1:4a,5).
   A. Don't go anywhere without the gift: "do not leave Jerusalem but wait" (v. 4a).
   B. What is the gift we are to wait for? "You will be baptized with the Holy Spirit" (v. 5).
   C. Jesus gave the command to wait for the baptism more than once (Lk 24:49).
   D. What does it mean to be baptized with the Holy Spirit?
      1. It means to be clothed with and filled with the power of the Spirit of God (Lk 24:49; Ac 1:8).

II. **THE REASON FOR CHRIST'S FINAL COMMAND** (Ac 1:4,5,8).
   A. The Father had promised the gift
      1. through the prophet (Joel 2:28-29).
      2. through John the Baptist (Mk 1:7-8).
   B. The gift of the Holy Spirit was a primary goal of Jesus' ministry.
      1. John the Baptist said that, when Jesus came, He would "baptize people with the Holy Spirit." (Mk 1:7-8)
      2. Jesus often spoke about this with His disciples (Ac 1:4) "which you have heard me speak about."
      3. John 7:37-39 is one instance of Jesus speaking about it.
   C. The gift is God's way to empower Christians to be His witnesses (Ac 1:8).
      1. Jesus commanded His disciples to go into all the world and make disciples of all nations (Mt 28:18-20).

2. Jesus commanded the disciples to seek the experience of the baptism in the Holy Spirit, because they needed His power to fulfill the commission.
3. God's commission for the church has not changed; therefore, we still need the power of the Holy Spirit to accomplish it.

III. WILL YOU OBEY CHRIST'S FINAL COMMAND?
A. Because the Spirit has come we are commanded to be Christ's witnesses (Jn 15:26-27).
B. If we love Him we will obey Him, and He will give us the Spirit to dwell in us and fill us with power (Jn 14:15-17).
C. God gives His Spirit to those who obey Him (Ac 5:32).
 1. The apostles were speaking about obeying Christ to witness.

Conclusion and Altar Call
Come in obedience to Christ's command and receive the power that He wants to give you to serve Him and be an effective witness.

[MT]

13. Fan Into Flame the Gift of God

Sermon in a Sentence: We must each experience continual, personal Pentecostal revival if we are to be effective Christians.
Sermon Purpose: That people may understand how they can be continually filled and refilled with the Holy Spirit, and that they be filled or refilled today
Text: 2 Timothy 1:6-8, 11-12, 14

Introduction
1. In our text Paul is telling Timothy how he can experience personal Pentecostal revival and why he needs to seek it.
2. He reminds Timothy to "fan into flames" the gift of God that was in him, the gift that he first received when Paul laid hands on him.
3. Paul is referring to the gift of the Spirit that Timothy received when he was baptized in the Holy Spirit.
4. This gift must be continually renewed.
5. We must do certain things to experience personal Pentecostal revival.
6. But first let's see how Paul defines revival in this passage.

I. **ACCORDING TO THIS TEXT, TO EXPERIENCE PERSONAL PENTECOSTAL REVIVAL MEANS THREE THINGS:**
   A. It means to be personally filled with the Spirit (2Ti 1:6b).
      1. The "gift of God" spoken of in this text is the baptism in Holy Spirit (Ac 1:4, 8:20, 11:17).
         a. In this context this is not a ministry gift.
         b. Paul also includes himself as having received this gift. ("God gave *us* a spirit …")
      2. Timothy was apparently filled with the Spirit when Paul laid hands on him and prayed for him.
         a. This possibly happened in the church in Lystra that Paul started (Ac 14:8-20, 16:1-3).
      3. Spirit baptism following salvation was the pattern in the New Testament church (Ac 8:15-17; 9:17; 19:6).
   B. It means to consciously allow the Spirit to operate in one's life (2Ti 1:7).
      1. The Spirit's presence and work brings change in our lives.
      2. In the place of fear He brings power (Ac 1:8).
      3. He brings love (Ro 5:5).
      4. He brings self-control (Gal 5:16).
   C. It means to be actively witnessing for Christ.
      1. "Do not be ashamed to testify about our Lord" (2 Ti 1:8).

2. This reminds us of Christ's words in Acts 1:8.

II. THREE REASONS WE NEED TO EXPERIENCE PERSONAL REVIVAL.
A. Because we will face opposition when we preach the Gospel (2Ti 1:8, 11-12).
B. Because we need the help of the Spirit to remain true to the gospel message and sound doctrine (2Ti 1:14).
C. Because of our tendency to lose zeal for serving Christ (2Ti 1:6a).
   1. Paul tells Timothy to "stir up," or "rekindle," or "fan into flame," the gift of God which was in him.
   2. A fire must be stirred and fed or it will eventually go out.
   3. Many had abandoned Paul and turned back (2 Ti 1:15; 4:10a).
   4. Paul was concerned that Timothy remain committed.
   5. We, too, must be vigilant to maintain our commitment to Christ and His mission by maintaining the presence of the Spirit in our lives.

III. TO EXPERIENCE PERSONAL PENTECOSTAL REVIVAL WE MUST DO SOMETHING.
A. Like Timothy, we must begin with a sincere faith in Christ (2Ti 1:5).
B. We must recognize that the Holy Spirit brings revival when we seek to be filled with His presence.
C. We must begin by ensuring that we have been filled.
   1. You can be filled today.
D. We must then continually fan into flame the gift of God.
   1. By believing the promise (Jn 7:37-39).
   2. By stepping out in faith and witnessing for Christ (Ac 5:32).
   3. By continually seeking God and asking to be filled (Lk 11:9-10, 13).

Conclusion and Altar Call
1. Let us come and pray that God will fill us with the Holy Spirit.
2. If you have never been filled before, the promise is for you. Come and let the fire be ignited in your life.
3. If you have already received the baptism in the Holy Spirit, come and fan the flame by being refilled so that you can continue to serve Christ and witness in the power of the Holy Spirit.

[MT]

14. Have You Received Since You Believed?

Sermon in a Sentence: You can receive the Holy Spirit as did the twelve disciples in Ephesus.

Sermon Purpose: That believers be filled and refilled with the Holy Spirit.

Text: Acts 19:1-7 (KJV)

Introduction
1. When Paul came into Ephesus he found a city filled with idolatry and immorality. (They worshiped Artemis, the many-breasted goddess of fertility.)
2. Paul's plan was to reach Ephesus, and all of Asia Minor, with the gospel (see Ac 19:10).
3. He began by asking a question:

I. PAUL'S QUESTION
A. Paul asked, "Have you received the Holy Spirit since you believed?"
B. Why did Paul ask this question? What made him think they had not received this promised gift? What were they doing that prompted the question?
   1. Perhaps it was their behavior or speech.
   2. Perhaps it was their worship.
   3. Perhaps Paul sensed it in his spirit.
   4. Although Paul regarded them as true believers, he knew that something more was needed in their lives.
   5. Their understanding and experience with the Holy Spirit was lacking.
C. Would someone recognize the Spirit in your life?

II. THE TWELVE DISCIPLES' RESPONSE
A. The twelve responded, "We've never even heard that there is a Holy Spirit!"
   1. They were not aware of the power the Spirit had to help them.
   2. Or of the gifts He had to give them.
   3. Or of the guidance that He had for them.
   4. They didn't even know that He was available!
B. How would you answer Paul's question?
   1. Would you answer like the Ephesians?
   2. Would your actions cause people to ask, "Have you received since you believed?"

        3. Do we, as professing Pentecostals, fully embrace the ministry of the Holy Spirit?
    C. Are you prepared to receive His power for living today?

III. PAUL'S ACTION
    A. He prayed with them to receive the Holy Spirit (Ac 19:6).
    B. They received the Holy Spirit just as the 120 disciples on the Day of Pentecost (Ac 2:1-4).
        1. This was 25 years after Pentecost.

IV. OUR RESPONSE TODAY
    A. We can receive the same experience today!
        1. In the same way (Ac 2:38-39).
        2. With the same evidence (Ac 2:4; 19:6).
        3. For the same purpose (Ac 1:8).
    B. But why do we need this experience?
        1. We live a corrupt society like that of Ephesus.
        2. We must have the Spirit's power to be effective witnesses for Christ.
        3. Further, we need the Spirit's power in order to have a deep intimate relationship with Christ—that Christ might be known and exalted in our lives.
    C. None of this will happen until we are first baptized in the Holy Spirit (Lk 24:49; Ac 1:4-8).
        1. It happened to the disciples at Pentecost.
        2. It happened to the twelve disciples in Ephesus.
        3. It can happen to you today.

Conclusion and Altar Call
    1. Prepare your heart before God.
    2. Come in faith and expectation.
    3. Ask God to fill you (Lk 11:13).

[KK]

15 The Holy Spirit Empowers

Sermon in a Sentence: If you will be baptized in the Holy Spirit you will receive power to be Christ's witness.
Sermon Purpose: That believers will understand and receive the transforming power of the Holy Spirit.
Text: Acts 1:8

Introduction
1. Now, as in the book of Acts, the power of Pentecost does more to cause the spreading of the gospel than any other single thing.
   a. It is no accident that the greatest missionary thrust in the world today comes from Pentecostals.
   b. And yet many misunderstand the nature of this experience.
   c. This misunderstanding hinders our witness to the world.
2. In this message we will seek to understand the nature and purpose of Pentecostal power.
3. Let's look at three things Jesus taught about the power of the Spirit in Acts 1:8:

I. **JESUS PROMISED THE SPIRIT'S PROVISION**
   A. What kind of power did Jesus promise in verse 8?
      1. He was not talking about authority (Greek: *exousia*, used in v. 7), but ability (Greek: *dunamis*, v. 8).
      2. Jesus was promising power to get the job done.
   B. Jesus knew that these believers were not ready to go out into the world in their own power or strength.
      1. He had already given them His authority (Lk 9:1); now they needed a power that could transform them.
      2. This power would empower them the way they needed in order to do the work Jesus had called them to do.
      3. We need this same power today.
   C. Spirit baptism is a real, noticeable experience.
      1. It is different and separate from salvation.
      2. These people had already received the Spirit in the new birth (Jn 20:22).
      3. They already had the Holy Spirit; the Holy Spirit would soon have them.
      4. We need this touch of the Spirit today as well.

II. **JESUS EXPLAINED THE DISCIPLES' NEW POSITION.**
   A. Jesus was promising *transformation*.
      1. Note that Jesus said that they would *be* His witnesses.
         a. The emphasis is not just on doing, but being.
         b. This includes a transformation of character.

      2. In Acts people ministered out of transformed lives.
         a. Peter is a prime example (Compare Mt 26:69-75 with Ac 2:14ff).
         b. The person is transformed ... not just the tongue.
      3. The Spirit's first work is to transform us.
         a. This is why the baptism of the Holy Spirit is so important for believers!
   B. Jesus was also concerned about *testimony.*
      1. The disciples' baptism resulted in powerful testimony.
      2. This testimony included
         a. Powerful proclamation (Ac 2:14-40).
         b. Powerful signs and wonders (Ac 2:43).
         c. Powerful community (Ac 2:44-47).
      3. All served as a powerful witness to the lost.

III. JESUS REVEALED THE SPIRIT'S PLACEMENT.
   A. This power will find its *tactical* (or strategic) expression.
      1. It Involves both placement and practice.
      2. The Spirit's power should make itself felt in four strategic places of witness:
         a. In our homes.
         b. In our village, town, or city ("Jerusalem").
         c. In neighboring towns and villages ("Judea and Samaria").
         d. In all the world ("to the ends of the earth").
      3. God takes His people, fills them with His power, and then scatters them in a world that desperately needs them.
   B. This power also relates to *time.*
      1. The Great Commission not only extends to the "ends of the earth" (Ac 1:8) but to the "end of the age" (Mt 28:20).
      2 This baptism of the Holy Spirit was not just for the first-century saints, it was meant for all believers, for all time, until Jesus comes again! (Ac 1:11; 3:19-20).
      3. It is meant for us today!
   C. At Pentecost "they were *all* filled with the Holy Spirit."
      1. They were *all* told to wait until the promise came.
      2. We too must "wait until we are clothed with power from on high" (Lk 24:49).

Conclusion and Altar Call
1. The Spirit will transform you into a witness for Christ.
2. He will change you so you can change your world.
3. Come now to be filled.

[DWM]

16. Jesus' Personal Instructions on Receiving the Spirit

Sermon in a Sentence: Jesus tells us how to receive the Holy Spirit.
Sermon Purpose: That believers receive the Holy Spirit.
Text: Luke 11:9-13

Introduction
1. Here, Jesus tells His disciples how they may receive the Holy Spirit.
2. Note that He is directing His teaching, not to sinners, but to disciples.
   a. v. 1 "disciples"
   b. v. 13 "sons"
3. Jesus gives us three instructions about receiving the Holy Spirit:

I. WE MUST ASK.
A. Three times we are instructed to "ask" (vv. 9, 10, 13)
B. Our asking must be in faith (Mk 11:24).
C. We ask, He gives, we receive by faith (vv. 9-10).

II. WE MUST BE SERIOUS.
A. Beyond asking, we must "seek" and "knock" (v. 9).
   1. This Implies seriousness on our part.
B. We must hunger and thirst after God (Mt 5:6; Jn 3:37).
C. ILLUS: Tell the story of the persistent friend (vv. 5-8).

III. WE MUST NOT BE AFRAID.
A. Some are afraid …
   1. … of God, that He will not receive them.
   2. … of a false or demonic experience.
   3. Here Jesus allays both fears.
B. Don't be afraid of God.
   1. Because He is a loving Heavenly Father.
C. Don't be afraid of a false experience, because God …
   1. … will not give you a snake if you ask for a fish.
   2. … will not give you a scorpion if you ask for an egg.
   3. … will not give you a false experience.

Conclusion and Altar Call
Come and receive the Spirit today.
   Ask and it will be given.
   Seek and you will find.
   Knock and the door will be opened.

[DRM]

17. Jesus, the Baptizer in the Holy Spirit

Sermon in a Sentence: Look to Jesus to be baptized in the Spirit.
Sermon Purpose: That believers will come to Jesus and be baptized in the Holy Spirit,
Text: Luke 3:16

I. **JESUS IS THE ONE WHO BAPTIZES IN THE HOLY SPIRIT.**
   A. We should look to Jesus, not only as our Savior and Healer, but also as our Baptizer in the Holy Spirit.
   B. The only sign of the Messiah mentioned in all four gospels is that He baptizes in the Holy Spirit (Mt 3:11; Mk 1:8; Lk 3:16; Jn 1:33).
   C. Look to Jesus today as your Baptizer in the Holy Spirit!

II. **WE MUST PREPARE OURSELVES TO RECEIVE THIS BAPTISM FROM JESUS.**
   A. We must prepare ourselves *spiritually* (Ac 2:38).
      1. We must be born again.
      2. We must confess and forsake any habitual sin.
   B. We must prepare ourselves *mentally*.
      1. We must not let misinformation confuse us.
      2. We must rather believe what the Bible teaches:
         a. The baptism in the Holy Spirit is available today (Ac 2:14-17).
         b. The baptism in the Holy Spirit is for all believers (Ac 3:38-39).
         c. Speaking in tongues as the Spirit gives utterance is the initial physical evidence of the baptism in the Holy Spirit (Ac 2:4).
         d. Many other wonderful results will follow (for example: power to witness, a closer relationship with God, gifts of the Spirit, power over demons, etc.).
         e. The experience must be maintained (Eph 5:18).
   C. We must prepare ourselves *emotionally*.
      1. Our hearts must be ready to receive.
      2. We must want to be baptized in the Holy Spirit (Mt 5:6; 6:33; Jn 7:37-39).
      3. We must believe that Jesus will baptize us in the Holy Spirit (Ac 1:4-5; Mk 11:24).

Conclusion and Altar Call
Come to Jesus and let Him baptize you today.

[JWL]

18. Jesus, Savior and Baptizer

Sermon in a Sentence: You can know Jesus today as your Savior and as your Baptizer in the Holy Spirit.

Sermon Purpose: That sinners might come to Christ and be saved and that believers might come to Christ and be empowered for witness.

Text: John 1:29-34

Introduction
1. In our text John the Baptist announced Jesus' two great redemptive roles: (He is ...)
   a. "the Lamb who takes away the sins of the world" (v. 29).
   b. "the One who baptizes in the Holy Spirit" (v. 33).
2. Today you should come to know Him as both *Savior and Baptizer!*
   a. He became our Savior at the Cross ... when He gave Himself as the sacrifice for the sins of all mankind.
   b. He became our Spirit-baptizer at Pentecost ... when He poured out His Spirit on His church to empower it to take the message of the cross to all mankind.
3. This message will look at both works of Jesus and at what they mean to us today.

I. **MEET JESUS, THE SAVIOR OF THE WORLD.**
   A. He is the Lamb of God.
      1. John's announcement: "Look, the Lamb of God ..." (Jn 1:29).
      2. As the Lamb of God Jesus is God's provision for our sins (1Jn 2:2; Jn 3:16).
      3. He wants all to be saved (2Pe 3:9).
   B. He died that we might have life.
      1. He died in our place (2Co 5:21).
      2. He died for all of us (1Jn 2:2).
   C. Receive Him as savior today. (How?)
      1. Through repentance and faith (Mk 1:15; Ac 20:21).
      2. *Repent* of your sins (Ac 3:19; Ac 17:30).
      3. Put your *faith* in Christ alone for salvation (Ac 16:31).

II. **MEET JESUS, THE BAPTIZER IN THE HOLY SPIRIT.**
   A. He is the giver of the Spirit.
      1. John's announcement: v. 33 "he will baptize with the..."
      2. As the Baptizer in the Holy Spirit He empowers His people to preach the message of salvation.
         a. Before Pentecost (Ac 1:8).

        b. At Pentecost (Ac 2:4, 41, 47).
        c. After Pentecost (Ac 4:31, 33).
    3. He wants all to hear (Lk 24:47).
B. He gave His Spirit that we might have power.
    1. All who have been saved have been commissioned as His witnesses (Lk 24:48).
    2. Therefore all who have been saved need His power (Lk 24:49).
    3. Therefore, He has commanded all to receive His Spirit (Ac 1:4-5).
C. Receive Him as Baptizer today. (How?)
    1. Ask in faith (Lk 11:9, 13).
    2. Receive by faith (Lk 11:10; Mk 11:24).
    3. Speak in faith (Ac 2:4; Jn 7:37-39).

Conclusion and Altar Call

Come to Jesus now as your Savior and Baptizer in the Holy Spirit!

                                                                [DRM]

19. Jesus Will Fill You with the Holy Spirit So You Can Witness

Sermon in a Sentence: Christ's priority for every believer is that they be filled with the Spirit and empowered to witness for Him.
Sermon Purpose: That believers be filled with power for witness
Text: Acts 1:8

Introduction
1. Jesus came to this earth for two primary purposes. John the Baptist announced those two purposes (Jn 1:29-34):
   a. To provide salvation and forgiveness of sins.
   b. To fill us with the Holy Spirit so we can preach the gospel.
2. According to Acts 1:8, the purpose of the baptism in the Holy Spirit is to give believers power to be witnesses for Christ.
3. Every born-again believer needs to be a witness for Christ and, therefore, needs to be filled with, and remain full of, the Spirit.
4. At the very end of Jesus' time on earth He repeatedly emphasized the priority of receiving the power of the Holy Spirit and witnessing for Him.
5. Let's look at three powerful facts that prove that Jesus' priority for every believer is to be filled with the Holy Spirit and begin to witness for Him.

I. THE NIGHT BEFORE JESUS WAS CRUCIFIED HE SPOKE ABOUT THE COMING OF THE SPIRIT AND HOW THE APOSTLES MUST WITNESS FOR HIM.
   A. On the night Jesus was betrayed He repeatedly talked with the apostles about the coming of the Holy Spirit and what the Spirit would do in them (Jn chapters 13-17).
   B. He said that they would do the same works that He did and even greater works (meaning more of them) because He was going to the Father (Jn 14:12).
      1. The significance is that He was going to the Father so the Spirit would come in His place (Jn 16:7-8).
   C. He promised to send them the Holy Spirit if they would obey His command (Jn 14:15-20).
      1. The command to wait in Jerusalem would come later after His resurrection.
      2. He said that the Spirit who was now with them would come into them (v. 17).
   D. Later in this passage Jesus spoke again about the coming of the Spirit. This time He told the disciples that as a result they must begin to witness (Jn 15:26).

II. **THE NIGHT OF HIS RESURRECTION JESUS COMMANDED HIS DISCIPLES TO BE FILLED WITH THE SPIRIT AND WITNESS** (Jn 20:19-22).
   A. On the day Jesus rose from the dead He appeared to the apostles, and the first thing He spoke to them about was their commission to be His witnesses (v. 21).
   B. He breathed on them and said, "Receive the Holy Spirit." (v. 22).
   C. We saw how just before His death Jesus spoke with His disciples about being filled with the Spirit and witnessing, and immediately after rising from the dead He does the same.

III. **BEFORE HE ASCENDED TO HEAVEN JESUS TWICE COMMANDED HIS FOLLOWERS TO NOT LEAVE JERUSALEM UNTIL THEY HAD BEEN BAPTIZED IN THE HOLY SPIRIT AND EMPOWERED FOR WITNESS** (Lk 24:46-49; Ac 1:4-5).
   A. Luke records both of these occasions when Jesus gave this command to His disciples. These were Jesus' last words and show His priority for His followers.
      1. Jesus' purpose for believers is that they witness for Him.
      2. That is why His priority for us is that we be filled with the Spirit, so we will have the power to fulfill His mission.
   B. If we love our Lord, we will listen and obey His command to seek the baptism in the Spirit.
   C. Those first disciples who heard Jesus repeatedly emphasize their need of the fullness of the Spirit obeyed His command and waited in Jerusalem (Ac 1:12, 14).
   D. Ten days later, on the Day of Pentecost, the promise was fulfilled and God poured out of the Holy Spirit on all those who obeyed and were seeking the power of the Spirit.
   E. After the disciples were filled with the Spirit at Pentecost, Peter proclaimed that this gift of the Spirit is now available to all who will repent and put their faith in Christ (Ac 2:38-39).

Conclusion and Altar Call
   1. Since that time Jesus has been looking for people who will believe and accept His gift of the Holy Spirit.
   2. If you will believe and be willing to commit your life to witnessing for Christ, you will be filled with the Holy Spirit as well.
   3. Come now in faith and begin to ask Jesus to fill you with the Holy Spirit.

[MT]

20 Living Water

Sermon in a Sentence: Christ has invited all who are thirsty for God's power and presence to come and be filled with His Spirit
Sermon Purpose: To see people baptized in the Holy Spirit
Text: John 7:37-39

Introduction
1. Many people long for a real spiritual experience, one that will satisfy their hearts and fill them with power, purpose, and peace.
2. They look in many places attempting to satisfy this desire.
3. In John 7 Jesus invites all who are looking for something to fill that empty longing in their life to come to Him and receive the gift which will truly satisfy.
4. Let's look at the invitation this Jesus has made (Jn 7:37-39):

I. JESUS OFFERED THE GIFT OF LIVING WATER.
  A. What is the gift?
    1. Living water is an image of the Holy Spirit (v. 39).
    2. Jesus is referring specifically to the outpouring of the Holy Spirit on the Day of Pentecost (v. 39).
    3. He invites us to come and drink (i.e., to receive the presence and power of the Spirit inside of us.)
    4. God had promised this gift: "I will *pour out* my Spirit" (Joel 2:28-29)
    5. Just before Jesus ascended to heaven He confirmed that the promise would soon be fulfilled (Ac 1:4-5).
    6. The gift of living water is a gift of God's power so that those who receive it can serve God's plan of building His kingdom (Ac 1:8).
    7. At Pentecost the living water was poured out (Ac 2:1-4).
  B. Who is the gift for?
    1. The gift of the Holy Spirit is for all people everywhere.
    2. Jesus said "if *anyone* is thirsty let him come", and again, "*whoever* believes in me".
    3. On the Day of Pentecost all who gathered were filled. Peter later announced that the gift was "for all whom the Lord our God will call" (Ac 2:39).
    4. The gift of the Spirit is for you. Receive it today.

II. THE RESULT OF RECEIVING THE GIFT OF LIVING WATER
  A. Living water satisfies the thirst of the soul.
    1. The water that Jesus offers is *living*. It is the gift of God's own Spirit who fills us with the life and power of Christ.
    2. The presence and work of the Spirit in us will result in …

        a. ... the fruit of the Spirit (Gal 5:22-23).
        b. ... power to overcome sin (Gal 5:16).
        c. ... assurance you are a child of God (Ro 8:15-16).
        d. ... a guarantee of our future redemption (Eph 1:13f).
  B. Living water fills us with the power to bless others (Jn 7:38).
    1. Streams of living water will flow from within.
    2. God's purpose in filling us is so that the power of the Spirit will overflow out of us bringing life to others.
    3. This is what Jesus was referring to in Acts 1:8.
    4. Christ wants your life to be a channel through which the Spirit can flow to bring life to those who are dead in sin.
  C. God's plan is that living water be a continual experience (Jn 7:38).
    1. The Spirit's presence is to be a continual flowing stream.
    2. This is why the New Testament constantly encourages us to walk in the Spirit and to live by the Spirit. (Gal 5:25: "Since we live by the Spirit, let us keep in step with the Spirit").
    3. There is nothing more important to your success in serving God than to be continually filled with the Spirit.

III. WE MUST GO TO THE SOURCE OF LIVING WATER.
  A. Jesus is the source: "Let him come to me" (Jn 7:37).
    1. He is the source because the Holy Spirit is His Spirit.
  B. Since Jesus is the source of the Spirit, we must go to Him to receive. He is the only one who can give the gift.
  C. Jesus said, "If you are thirsty, come to me."
    1. How do we do that? By faith in Him.
    2. Jesus said "Whoever believes in me"
  D. Lastly, we must believe that He will fill us with the Holy Spirit.
    1. Jesus openly invites anyone to come to Him and drink. He wants to fill us.
    2. Take Jesus at His word. Believe Him and reach out to Him and He will fill you.

Conclusion and Altar Call

If you are thirsty for God, the invitation to come and drink is for you. Come and be filled today.

[MT]

21 The Most Important Thing in the Church Today

Sermon in a Sentence: The baptism in the Holy Spirit is a vital experience for every Christian.
Sermon Purpose: That believers will be baptized in the Holy Spirit.
Text: Acts 1:1-8

Introduction
1. What is the most important thing in the church today?
2. The most important thing in the church today is that every member be powerfully baptized in the Holy Spirit.

I. **FIVE REASONS I BELIEVE THAT THE BAPTISM IN THE HOLY SPIRIT IS THE MOST IMPORTANT THING IN THE CHURCH TODAY.**
   A. It was Jesus' last message to the Church.
      1. Jesus could have talked about many things…
         a. Church growth, relationships, tithing…
      2. He chose to talk about the necessity of being empowered by the Spirit (Ac 1:8).
   B. It was Paul's first message to the twelve Ephesian disciples (Ac 19:1-7).
      1. Paul's plan was reach Ephesus and all of Asia Minor with the gospel (Ref. Ac 19:10.).
      2. Paul's first message to the Ephesian disciples was, "Did you received the Holy Spirit when you believed?"
      3. If they were going to participate in reaching Ephesus and Asia Minor, they needed to be empowered by the Spirit.
   C. Even Mary, the mother of Jesus, needed to be baptized in the Holy Spirit.
      1. Before Pentecost she waited with the others to receive the Spirit (Ac 1:13-14).
      2. Remember, she was specially chosen of all women to bear the Christ (Lk 1:28, 35).
      3. If she still needed to be baptized in the Holy Spirit, how much more do we.
   D. It is the one promise in the Bible referred to as *the* Promise of the Father.
      1. Read: Acts 1:4 (NKJV). Note the word "the."
      2. Indicates that the baptism in the Holy Spirit is a special and important experience from God.
   E. Jesus Himself chose to minister only through the power and anointing of the Holy Spirit.

  1. He was empowered at His water baptism (Lk 3:21-22), then, in the next verse: "He began His ministry."
  2. He began His ministry in the power of the Spirit (Lk 4:14,16-19).
  3. He performed His ministry in the power of the Spirit (Ac 10:38).
  4. He did it in this way in order that He might be an example for our ministries (Jn 14:26).
 F. Each of these facts demonstrates the importance of the baptism in the Holy Spirit.

II. A QUESTION: WHY IS THE BAPTISM IN THE HOLY SPIRIT SO IMPORTANT TO EVERY CHRISTIANS LIFE?
 A. It is the Christian's source of power for life and service (Ac 1:8).
  1. Jesus last command: "Stay in the city until you are clothed with power from on high" (Lk 24:49; Ac 1:4-5).
 B. Being baptized in the Holy Spirit will affect every area of your Christian life.
  1. Your witness for Christ (Ac 1:8; 4:31).
  2. Your understanding of the Word (Jn 14;26, 16:13).
  3. Your love for God and others (Ro 5:5).
  4. The way you worship God (Jn 4:23).
  5. Your prayer life (Ro 8:26-27).
  6. Your victory over temptation and sin (Ro 8:4-8).

III. HERE IS HOW YOU CAN BE FILLED TODAY.
 A. Ask God to fill you (Lk 10:9,13).
 B. Receive the gift by faith (Lk 11:10; Mk 11:24).
 C. Sense His presence coming upon you and filling you (Ac 10:44).
 D. Speak out in faith allowing the Spirit to speak through you (Ac 2:4).

Conclusion and Altar Call
 1. The baptism in the Holy Spirit is the most important experience a Christian can receive.
 2. Come now to be filled with the Spirit.

[DRM]

22. Our Generous God

Sermon in a Sentence: God generously gives His Spirit to anyone who asks.
Sermon Purpose: That believers will be filled with the Spirit and committed to preaching the gospel to all people.
Text: Acts 10:34-47

Introduction
1. Our text tells the story of God's generous outpouring of His Spirit on the Gentiles.
2. It centers around two people: Peter, a Jew, and Cornelius, a Gentile.
   a. The Spirit prepared both men for their meeting:
   b. He prepared Cornelius' faith.
   c. He dealt with Peter's prejudices.
3. This story demonstrates the great generosity of our God in three ways:

I. GOD SHOWS PARTIALITY TO NO PERSON OR PEOPLE.
A. God taught Peter this lesson.
  1. He gave Peter a vision (Ac 10:9-16).
  2. Peter's conclusion: "God has shown me that I should not call any man impure or unclean" (v. 28).
B. We should never forget that God loves everyone.
  1. He does not favor one group over another.
  2. He loves both Jews and Gentiles.
  3. He loves even those who reject Him.
  4. Thank God, He has generously included you and me.
C. Therefore, we who represent God should show no partiality.
  1. We must love all people.
  2. We must generously share the gospel with all people.

II. GOD POURS OUT HIS SPIRIT ON ALL PEOPLE.
A. In our story God poured His Spirit out on all who were present—both Jews and Gentiles.
  1. Peter told them of how God had anointed Jesus with the Holy Spirit (v. 38).
  2. Then, "while Peter was still speaking these words, the Holy Spirit came on *all* who heard the message" (v. 44). (This included the Jewish brothers with Peter as well as the many Gentiles gathered at Cornelius' house.)
  3. The Jewish men were amazed that God had poured out the Spirit "even on the Gentiles" (v. 45).

   4. They knew the Gentiles had been filled because "they heard them speaking with tongues and magnifying God."
  B. Notice how the power of the Spirit is very practical:
   1. Jesus "went around doing good and healing all who were under the power of the devil" (v. 38).
   2. Peter, who was once fearful, is now preaching with power.
   3. This is according to Jesus' promise in Acts 1:8.
  C. When we are baptized in the Holy Spirit we receive power …
   1. … to preach the gospel to all.
   2. … to perform miracles, healings, and deliverances.
   3. … to plant churches.

III. GOD COMMANDS US TO PREACH TO ALL PEOPLE.
  A. In his sermon Peter said,
   1. "We are witnesses of everything he did" (v. 39).
   2. "He commanded us to preach to the people and to testify that he is the one whom God appointed as judge of the living and the dead" (v. 42).
  B. We are Christ's witnesses to all people (Ac 1:8).
   1. We must preach the gospel to *all people*.
   2. We must preach the gospel in *every place*.
  C. Because all will be judged, all must hear the truth (v. 42).
   1. We do not have forever to accomplish the task—Jesus is coming!
   2. We must preach the gospel now.
   3. We must go in the power of the Holy Spirit (Ac 1:8).

Conclusion and Altar Call
  1. Come and be filled that you may receive power to take the gospel to the lost.
  2. Our generous God will graciously pour out His Spirit on you today.

[EL]

23. The Power of the Promise

Sermon in a Sentence: We must each receive the promise of the Holy Spirit as prophesied by the prophet Joel.
Sermon Purpose: That believers will be filled with the Holy Spirit.
Text: Joel 2:28-29

Introduction
1. What would you rather be: healthy or undernourished, impoverished or living in abundance, whole or incomplete, uninformed or knowledgeable, prepared or unequipped, ineffective or a powerful force against the devil?
2. Our text speaks to these important issues.
3. Joel prophesied the coming of the Holy Spirit on all flesh.
4. Let's look at that promise in three ways:

I. **THE PROMISE IN SACRED HISTORY**
   A. In the Old Testament Pentecost was known as the "Feast Weeks" (Ex 34:22).
      1. It happened fifty days after the Feast of Passover.
      2. Pentecost means "fifty."
   B. It was also called the Feast of First Fruits (Ex 23:16, 19).
      1. It celebrated the dedication of the first fruits of the barley harvest.
      2. At Pentecost God first empowered the church for a different type of harvest—a worldwide harvest of souls for God's kingdom (Ac 1:4-5, 8; 2: 1-13).
   C. Pentecost was a fulfillment of Joel's Prophecy (Joel 2:28-29)
      1. Peter quoted Joel at Pentecost (Ac 2:17-18).
      2. Today our receiving the Spirit will result in …
         a. … prophetic gifts in operation.
         b. … an overflowing fullness of the Spirit.
         c. … holiness, obedience, and righteousness.
         d. … a deeper reverence for God.
         e. … a greater consecration to God and His work.
         f. … a more active love for Jesus, His Word, and the lost and,
         g. … power to witness and live the Christian life.
   D. As a result of being filled with the Spirit, the disciples spoke in a new language (Ac 2:4; 10:46; 19:6).
      1. We can expect to do the same today.
      2. It is a sign that we have been anointed as Christ's Spirit-empowered witnesses (Ac 1:8).

II. THE PROMISE IN RECENT HISTORY
A. God began pouring out His Spirit anew in 1906 at a place called the Azusa Street Mission in Los Angeles, California, USA.
   1. The revival was lead by an African American preacher named William J. Seymour.
   2. He preached on the baptism in the Holy Spirit.
   3. The result was the great "Azusa Street Revival"
B. The revival that began at Azusa spread around the world.
   1. Today more than 600 million worldwide embrace the promise of the Spirit.

Editor's note: You can read the history of William J. Seymour and the Azusa Street Outpouring and how it impacted Africa in the book, *From Azusa to Africa to the Nations.* This book can be downloaded for free from the Decade of Pentecost website: http://www.decadeofpentecost.org/e-books.htm

III. THE PROMISE IN PERSONAL HISTORY
A. We must each make the promise of the Holy Spirit a part of our own personal history.
B. If we will do this, great benefits will come to our lives, such as,
   1. Power over demons (Mt 12:28; Eph 6:12).
   2. Greater sensitivity to the Spirit (Isa 30:21).
   3. More powerful witness for Christ.
      a. Power for witness is the chief purpose for the baptism in the Holy Spirit (Ac 1:8).
      b. Christ wants us to be His witness in every area of our lives.
      c. We are to become so identified with Christ that He is seen in us by all we come in contact with!

Conclusion and Altar Call
1. We each need the Spirit's power to transform and empower us as Christ's witnesses.
2. We each need our own personal Pentecost.
3. Come now and receive the "Power of the Promise" in your own life today.

[KK]

24. Prayer That Brings Down the Spirit

Sermon in a Sentence: We can pray in such a way that will bring the Spirit down into our lives and into our church services resulting in powerful Spirit-inspired witness.

Sermon Purpose: That believers would pray to God and experience the power of His Spirit giving them boldness to witness for Christ.

Text: Acts 4:23-31

Introduction
1. In Acts prayer is intimately connected with receiving the Spirit. (Examples: Ac 1:14; 8:17; 9:11; 10:2, 9; 19:6)
2. Our text is the only recorded instance in Acts where the content of believers' prayer for the Spirit is revealed.
3. It was a prayer that brought down a mighty outpouring of the Spirit on the people, resulting in the church being empowered and multitudes coming to the Lord.
4. Let's look more closely at this mighty prayer:

I. IT WAS A "EVERYONE-PARTICIPATING" PRAYER.
A. The prayer was not lead by one person while everyone else gave their silent consent.
B. Every person was an active participant in the prayer (v. 24).
C. If we are to see the Spirit poured out powerfully in our midst we must all be involved in prayer.

II. IT WAS A GOD-CENTERED PRAYER.
A. Unlike much of our praying today that focuses on our own personal wants and problems, their prayer focused on the power and sovereignty of God (vv. 24b-25).
B. Prayer that brings down the power of the Spirit is God-centered prayer.

III. IT WAS A CHRIST-HONORING PRAYER.
A. At the heart of their prayer was the will and work of Christ (vv. 26-28).
B. Prayer that brings down the Spirit focuses on the will and work of Christ.

IV. IT WAS A MISSION-ORIENTED PRAYER.
A. They did not ask for deliverance but for boldness to fulfill the mission of God (v. 29).
B. Prayer that brings God's Spirit into our lives and into our church services is mission-oriented prayer.

V. IT WAS A SPIRIT-INVOKING PRAYER.
   A. Their prayer called on the Spirit to manifest His power and presence through signs and wonders.
      1. These signs confirmed the gospel they were boldly proclaiming (v. 30).
      2. Note: The "hand of God" is a reference to the Holy Spirit (see: Eze 31:1; Lk 11:20; Ac 13:11).
   B. We should boldly ask the Spirit of God to fill us and manifest His power in our midst.

VI. IT WAS A FAITH-FILLED PRAYER.
   A. They fully expected that God would hear and answer their prayer.
   B. Prayer that brings down the Spirit of God is faith-filled prayer.

VII. IT WAS A GOD-ANSWERED PRAYER.
   A. God answered their prayer by manifesting His power and presence and by filling them with His Spirit, resulting in bold, Spirit-empowered witness (vv. 31, 33).
   B. We, too, can expect God to answer our prayer, send His Spirit, and empower us as His witnesses.

Conclusion and Altar Call
Come, let's pray that the Spirit will fill each of us today.

[DRM]

25. The Promise Fulfilled

Sermon in a Sentence: You can receive the promise of the Holy Spirit and be empowered to do the work of Jesus.
Sermon Purpose: That believers might be filled with the Spirit and empowered to work for God.
Texts: Judges 3:10-11; Joel 2:28-29; Acts 1:5

Introduction
1. In the Old Testament God's Spirit came upon special people at special times for special purposes.
2. Four examples from the book of Judges:
   a. Othniel (Jdg 3:10)
   b. Gideon (Jdg 6:34)
   c. Jephthah (Jdg 11:2)
   d. Samson (Jdg 13:25; 14:6; 14:19; 15:14)
3. The Spirit was given to them to enable them to do the work that God had given to them to do.

I. **THE PROPHETS PROMISED A DAY WHEN GOD WOULD POUR OUT HIS SPIRIT ON ALL FLESH.**
   A. The promise to Joel (Joel 2:28-29).
   B. The promise of John the Baptist (Lk 3:15-16).
   C. The promise of Jesus Himself (Ac 1:5).

II. **THE PROMISE WAS FIRST FULFILLED ON THE DAY OF PENTECOST** (Ac 2:1-4).
   A. Note how . . .
      1. The Spirit came upon them all (Ac 2:4).
      2. They were all filled with the Spirit and spoke in tongues as the Spirit enabled them (Ac 2:4).
      3. They became powerful witnesses for Jesus (Ac 2:14ff).
   B. The lesson: What the Lord promises He fulfills!

III. **THE PROMISE WAS FULFILLED AGAIN AND AGAIN THROUGHOUT THE BOOK OF ACTS.**
   A. It is for all of God's people (Ac 2:28-29).
   B. It is for all places (Ac 1:8).
      1. The promise was fulfilled again in Samaria (Ac 8:17-18).
      2. ... then again in Caesarea (Ac 10:44-46).
      3. ... then again in Ephesus (Ac 19:6).
   C. Each outpouring resulted in powerful missionary witness.

IV. **THE PROMISE WAS FULFILLED AT AZUSA STREET.**
   A. The story of the Azusa Street Outpouring.

B. It was the beginning of the modern Pentecostal movement.
  C. It launched a worldwide missionary movement.
  D. It quickly spread to Africa.

V. THE PROMISE IS NOW BEING FULFILLED ACROSS AFRICA.
  A. Many thousands are being filled.
  B. The promise is being filled here in _____.
  C. As a result, the church is becoming a powerful witnessing force.

VI. THE PROMISE IS FOR YOU TODAY.
  A. Jesus commands each of us to wait for the promise (Ac 1:4).
  B. We must each have this power to preach the gospel until Jesus comes again.
  C. Now it is your turn.
      1. Receive the promise today (Ac 2:38-39).
      2. Then boldly preach the gospel (Ac 1:8).

Conclusion and Altar Call
  1. Come now to see the promise fulfilled in your life.
  2. Ask and you will receive (Lk 11:9-10).
  3. If you believe you will see the glory of God.

[DM]

26. The Promise of Pentecost

Sermon in a Sentence: If we are going to do God's work, we must do it God's way, that is, in the power of the Holy Spirit.
Sermon Purpose: That believers might be empowered to do God's work.
Texts: Joel 2:28-31; Acts 1:4-8; 2:1-4

Introduction
1. God has given us a work to do.
2. He has also given us the power to do that work, that is the power of Pentecost.
3. This message will look at the promise of Pentecost.

I. THE PROMISE OF PENTECOST GIVEN
   A. Joel prophesied that the Spirit would one day be poured out on all people (Joel 2:28-29).
      1. The phrase, "poured out," reminds us of a heavy shower.
      2. The phrase, "all flesh," indicates that the promise includes old and young, men and women, rich and poor.
   B. Jesus restated the promise of Pentecost (Lk 24:49).
   C. If God makes a promise, we can be sure that He will fulfill it (Num 23:19).

II. THE PROMISE OF PENTECOST FULFILLED
   A. The Promise of Pentecost was first fulfilled on the Day of Pentecost (Ac 2:1-4).
      1. Peter said, "This is that" (Ac 2:16, KJV).
   B. The promise was fulfilled again and again throughout the book of Acts (Ac 4:8; 4:31; 8:17-18; 9:17-18; 10:44-46; 19:6).
   C. God wants to fulfill His promise again and again today.

III. THE RESULTS OF RECEIVING THE PROMISE OF PENTECOST
   A. They were all baptized in the Holy Spirit.
      1. To "baptize" means to totally immerse.
      2. Like immersing a cloth in dye until it becomes the color of the solution.
      3. The disciples were totally changed by the experience.
      4. We, too, will be changed by the Spirit.
   B. The following changes will occur:
      1. We will speak in tongues (Ac 2:4).
      2. We will receive power to witness (Ac 1:8; 2:40-41, 47).
      3. We will be used by the Spirit in miraculous manifestations (Ac 2:43).

4. We will begin to develop a Christ-like character (Gal 5:22-23).
   5. Gifts of the Spirit will be manifested in our lives (1Co 12:8-10).
   6. We will have a growing ministry, empowered by the Holy Spirit (as happened in the book of Acts).

IV. SUSTAINING THE PROMISE OF PENTECOST
   A. The Spirit-filled life must be sustained.
      1. We must learn to walk in step with the Spirit (Gal 5:25).
      2. We must cultivate a close relationship with God.
   B. We must receive many continued fillings with the Holy Spirit.
      1. See: Acts 2:4; 4:8; 31; 13:9.
      2. Eph 5:18 teaches that we must be repeatedly filled with the Holy Spirit. (Note: The phrase "be filled" is in the Greek continuous present tense)
   C. Evidences of a Spirit-filled life include…
      1. … a spirit of yieldedness.
      2. … a continued practice of prayer in tongues (1Co 14:18).
      3. … a miracle quality of life.
      4. … a miracle quality of ministry.
      5. … a life of empowered witness (Ac 1:8).

Conclusion and Altar Call
   1. We must each receive the Promise of the Spirit today.
   2. Come, ask, and receive by faith (Lk 11:8-13).

[JI and NO]

Adapted from "Lesson 4: Baptism in the Holy Spirit (Pentecost)" in *The Relevance of the Holy Spirit in Today's Church* by Rev. Dr. John O. Ikoni and Rev. Neubueze O. Oti., (Aba, Nigeria: Assemblies of God Press, 2009).

27. The Promise of the Holy Spirit

Sermon in a Sentence: We should all receive the promise of the Holy Spirit today.

Sermon Purpose: That believers understand and receive the promise of the Spirit, the baptism in the Holy Spirit.

Text: Acts 1:4-5: 2:33

Introduction
1. Our texts describe the baptism in the Holy Spirit as the "promise" of the Holy Spirit.
2. This powerful spiritual experience distinguishes the Pentecostal movement today, and is largely responsible for its creation and its tremendous growth worldwide.
3. Today we will learn about this powerful spiritual experience—this promise of the Holy Spirit.
4. Then, we will come to experience it for ourselves.

I. THE PERSON OF THE HOLY SPIRIT
A. The Holy Spirit is not an impersonal force, influence, or feeling; He is, rather, God Himself, the Third Person of the Godhead (Mt 28:19; Jn 14:16-17; 2Cor 13:14).
B. The baptism in the Holy Spirit is, therefore, a personal encounter with a personal God.
   1. Through Spirit baptism a believer is immersed in, and enveloped by, the person of the Holy Spirit (Lk 24:49).
   2. *He*, the Spirit of God, empowers *you*, the child of God.

II. THE PROMISE OF THE HOLY SPIRIT
A. Note how Jesus called the baptism in the Holy Spirit *the* promise—not just *a* promise—of the Father (Ac 1:4).
   1. It was promised in the Old Testament (Joel 2:28-29).
   2. It was prophesied by John the Baptist (Lk 3:16).
   3. It was announced by Jesus (Ac 1:4-8).
B. The baptism in the Holy Spirit is so important that...
   1. ... Jesus said it was better for His disciples that the Spirit come in His place than for Him to remain with them (Jn 16:7).
   2. ... it was Jesus' final command to His disciples, given with His Great Commission to evangelize the world (Lk 24:49; Ac 1:4-8).

III. THE PURPOSE OF THE BAPTISM IN THE HOLY SPIRIT
A. What the baptism in the Holy Spirit is *not* for:
   1. It is not for salvation.

      2. It is not for feeling or physical demonstrations.
      3. It is not simply for speaking in tongues. (Note: When you are filled with the Spirit you should expect to speak in tongues; and yet, tongues should not be viewed as the end or purpose of the experience.)
  B. Four benefits of the baptism in the Holy Spirit.
      1. It makes Christ more real.
      2. It makes God's Word more precious.
      3. It makes the fruit of the Spirit more pronounced.
      4. It opens the door to supernatural gifts and ministry enablement (1Co 12-14; Gal 3:5; Heb 2:3-4).
  C. The PRIMARY PURPOSE of the baptism in the Spirit is power to be Christ's witnesses (Lk 24:49; Ac 1:8).
      1. That is, to speak about Christ to the lost, and to show Him to the world by demonstrating His power and lordship in our lives.
      2. Jesus linked the baptism in the Holy Spirit to the Great Commission to evangelize the world (Ac 1:8).

IV. THE PROVISION FOR THE BAPTISM IN THE HOLY SPIRIT
  A. The promise has never been revoked; all of God's children can still be filled with the Spirit (Ac 2:38-39).
  B. Not only *can* all receive the promise, all *should* receive the promise of the Holy Spirit (Lk 24:49; Gal 3:14).
      1. All have been called to be Christ witnesses (Lk 24:46-48).
      2. Therefore, we must all receive the Spirit's power (Lk 24:49; Ac 1:8).

Conclusion and Altar Call
Come and receive the promise of the Spirit today.

[MS]

28. The Purpose of Pentecost

Sermon in a Sentence: We must each be filled with the Holy Spirit with a clear understand *why* God wants to fill us.
Sermon Purpose: That believers receive the Holy Spirit and understand the reason why God gives them the Spirit.
Text: Acts 1:8

Introduction
1. Many have been filled with the Holy Spirit without really understanding the purpose of the experience.
2. As a result, they are not used by God as He wants to use them.
3. In this message we will discuss the purpose of Pentecost.
4. But first we will discuss …

I. **WHAT THE BAPTISM IN THE HOLY SPIRIT IS NOT**
   A. It is not an achievement to boast about.
      1. Or a trophy to put on display.
      2. Or a toy to play with.
      3. Or a treasure to hoard.
   B. It is not a stepping stone to an official position in the church.
      1. That is, something that opens the door for eligibility to preach or teach.
      2. This would be a wrong reason to seek the experience.
   C. It is not a panacea, or cure-all, for our spiritual ills.
      1. Your problems will not automatically go away.
      2. You will not suddenly become a "super-spiritual" person.
   D. It is not the apex of Christian experience.
      1. Nor is it the ultimate goal of Christian endeavor.
      2. It is rather a means to a great end.
   E. It is not a permanent privilege so a person can call himself or herself "Pentecostal."
      1. Or a license to say, "Now I have the Holy Spirit!"
      2. The experience must be maintained.

II. **WHAT THE BAPTISM IN THE HOLY SPIRIT IS**
   A. It is a divine enablement to be a witness for Christ (Ac 1:8).
      1. Jesus called it a "clothing with power from on high" (Lk 24:49).
      2. It empowers us to be bold, active participants in God's work.
   B. It is a gateway into the dynamic gifts of the Holy Spirit.
      1. We must first receive the gift of the Holy Spirit (Ac 2:38-39).

        2. Then, we must manifest the gifts of the Spirit (1Co 12:8-10).
    C. It is the threshold over which one passes from ordinary to extraordinary living.
        1. From the usual to the unusual.
        2. From the natural to the supernatural.
    D. It is the "miracle-mantle" of the risen Christ fallen on the shoulders of His servants.
        1. Such a mantle rested on the ministry of Jesus (Lk 4:18; Ac 10:38).
        2. He passed His ministry on to His disciples (Jn 20:21-22).
            a. They received the power at Pentecost (Ac 2:1-4)
            b. Then they went out and ministered in miracle-working power.

Conclusion and Altar Call
1. You can receive that same Holy Spirit today.
2. Come and be filled now.

[WC]

*Adapted from William Caldwell's book *Pentecostal Baptism*, published by the author, 1963, pages 37-39.

29. Receive the Holy Spirit

Sermon in a Sentence: We must each receive the Holy Spirit today and become Christ's witnesses.

Sermon Purpose: That every believer present receives the Holy Spirit and becomes a witness for Christ.

Text: John 20:21-22

Introduction
1. This event took place on the night of Jesus' resurrection (Jn 20:1).
2. Jesus appeared to His disciples and did two significant things.
   a. He commissioned them (v. 21).
   b. He breathed on them and told them to receive the Spirit (v. 22).
3. From these two verses we learn three things about receiving the Spirit:

I. WE LEARN ABOUT THE IMPORTANCE OF RECEIVING THE SPIRIT.
   A. This is indicated by the fact that this was Jesus' very first message to His church after His resurrection.
   B. Note also that His last command before He returned to heaven was about receiving the Holy Spirit (Lk 24:49; Ac 1:4-8).
      1. Every believer is commanded to be filled with the Spirit (Eph 5:18).
      2. It is important for every believer to be filled with the Spirit because every believer has been commissioned as Christ's witness.

II. WE LEARN ABOUT THE PURPOSE OF RECEIVING THE SPIRIT.
   A. Notice the context of Jesus' breathing on His disciples:
      1. The context is commissioning for mission.
      2. "As the Father has sent me, I am sending you."
      3. This reminds us of Acts 1:8.
   B. If we are to be sent by Jesus as He was sent by the Father, we must be filled with the Spirit as He was filled with the Spirit (Lk 3:22-23; 4:17-18; Ac 10:38).
   C. We must all be empowered to participate in Christ's mission of reaching the lost at home and around the world.

III. WE LEARN ABOUT HOW EASY IT IS TO RECEIVE THE SPIRIT.

A. Jesus' act of breathing on the disciples is full of symbolism.
   1. He did more than just breathe air on them, He breathed the Spirit "into" them.
   2. (Note: The Gk. word *en,* translated "on," can also be translated "into.")
B. Just as breathing is normal thing for our physical man, being filled with the Spirit is normal for our spiritual man.
   1. For our natural man: breathing is normal—everyone does it!
   2. For our spiritual man: being filled with the Spirit is normal—every Christian should do it.
      a. It is the means by which our spiritual lives are sustained.
      b. The Spirit-filled life should not be the exception; it should be the normal state for Christians.
   3. Someone once said, "Many of us have lived sub-normal for so long that we think normal is abnormal."
C. Being filled with the Spirit is "as easy as breathing."
   1. Breathing is not only normal—*it is easy.*
   2. It takes no special effort for us to breath because our bodies were created to breath.
   3. It is also very easy to be filled with the Spirit because your spirit was created to receive the Holy Spirit.
   4. It requires no extraordinary effort on the part of the seeker.
   5. Listen to the promises of Jesus:
      a. Luke 11:13 "The heavenly Father will give the Holy Spirit to those who ask."
      b. v. 9: "Ask and it will be given you."
      c. v. 10 "Everyone who asks receives"
   6. We receive the Spirit by a simple act of faith.
D. You can be filled with the Spirit today by taking these three simple steps of faith:
   1. Ask in Faith (Lk 11:9, 13).
   2. Receive by Faith (Lk 11:10; Mk 11:24).
   3. Speak in Faith (Ac 2:4).

Conclusion and Altar Call
Come now and "breathe" in the Holy Spirit.

[DRM]

30. Receiving the Fullness of the Spirit

Sermon in a Sentence: You can receive the fullness of the Spirit by faith.

Sermon Purpose: That believers receive the Spirit with a clear understanding of the meaning and purpose of the experience.

Text: Acts 1:4-8; 2:4

Introduction
1. Our two texts use four phrases to describe the coming of the Holy Spirit to empower believers for service:
   a. Acts 1:5 they would be *"baptized in"* the Holy Spirit.
   b. Acts 1:8 the Holy Spirit would *"come upon"* them.
   c. Acts 1:8 they would *"receive"* power.
   d. Acts 2:4 they were all *"filled with"* the Holy Spirit.
2. This message will examine these four phrases.
3. We will then come to receive the Spirit in His fullness.

I. THE SPIRIT "COMES UPON" BELIEVERS.
   A. In Acts there are four examples:
      1. Jesus promised power when the Holy Spirit came upon the disciples (Ac 1:8).
      2. The Spirit came upon the Samaritan believers (Ac 8:16).
      3. The Spirit came upon the Caesareans (Ac 10:46).
      4. The Spirit came upon the Ephesian disciples (Ac 19:6).
   B. What do we learn from these instances?
      1. This reminds us of how the Spirit came upon the Old Testament prophets to inspire them to prophesy.
      2. God intends for His church to be a community of Spirit-anointed prophets (compare Num 11:24; Ac 2:17-18).
   C. How must we respond to these truths?
      1. When you come, expect the Spirit to come upon you.
      2. He will come upon you to empower you to be one of Jesus' Spirit-anointed witnesses.

II. THE SPIRIT "FILLS" BELIEVERS.
   A. The phrase "filled with the Spirit" is used five times in Acts:
      1. On the Day of Pentecost (Ac 2:4).
      2. Peter was again filled with the Spirit (Ac 4:8).
      3. There was a second Jerusalem outpouring (Ac 4:31, 33).
      4. Paul was filled with the Spirit (Ac 9:17).
      5. Paul was again filled with the Spirit (Ac 13:9).
   B. What do these passages teach us?
      1. Each time believers were filled with the Spirit they spoke for God as the Spirit inspired them.

       2. They were filled again and again.
   C. How must we respond to these truths?
       1. The Spirit will fill you so you can speak for Him.
       2. We should ask God to fill us again and again.

III. BELIEVERS ARE "BAPTIZED IN" THE HOLY SPIRIT.
   A. There are three examples in Acts:
       1. John the Baptist prophesied it (Lk 3:16).
       2. Jesus predicted it for His followers (Ac 1:5).
       3. Peter remembered the words of Jesus (Ac 11:16).
   B. What can we learn from these passages?
       1. Through Spirit baptism we are immersed in the presence and power of God.
       2. Further, we are initiated into God's mission of reaching the nations with the gospel.
   C. What must we do in response to these facts?
       1. Remember, when you receive the Spirit you will be initiated into God's army of Spirit-filled witnesses.

IV. BELIEVERS MUST "RECEIVE" THE SPIRIT.
   A. Receiving the Spirit is mentioned five times in Acts:
       1. Jesus described the experience (Ac 1:8).
       2. All believers can receive the gift of the Spirit (2:38-39).
       3. Paul received the Spirit (Ac 9:15-17).
       4. The Caesarean believers received the Spirit (Ac 10:47).
       5. The Ephesian disciples received the Spirit (Ac 19:2).
   B. What truths do we learn from these passages?
       1. Everyone who asks can expect to receive (Lk 10:10).
       2. Receiving the Spirit is an act of faith (Mk 11:24).
   C. What must we do in response to these passages?
       1. We can receive the Spirit by faith.
       2. Together we will take three steps of faith.
          a. We will ask in faith (Lk 10:9, 13).
          b. We will receive by faith (Lk 10:10; Mk 11:24).
          c. We will speak in faith (Ac 2:4; Jn 7:37).

Conclusion and Altar Call
Come now and receive the Spirit's fullness.

[DRM]

31 The Spirit on All Flesh

Sermon in a Sentence: Because God is pouring out His Spirit on all flesh, He will give His Spirit to everyone here today.
Sermon Purpose: That believers will realize that the Spirit is for them and that they receive the Spirit today.
Text: Joel 2:28-29; Acts 2:17-18

Introduction
1. Joel 2 has been called the "Pentecostal chapter" of the Old Testament.
2. Peter quoted this chapter to give scriptural basis for the happenings on the Day of Pentecost.
3. Let's discuss what this passage teaches about the outpouring of the Spirit

I. FEATURES OF THE OUTPOURING
A. It is a last-days awakening.
   1. Peter changed Joel's "afterward" to "last days" (Ac 2:17).
   2. The prophet indicates that there would be a special time of fulfillment during times of great distress.
   3. This describes the day in which we live.
B. The supernatural element of the awakening is emphasized.
   1. Note: "God says I will pour out my Spirit on all *flesh*" (Ac 2:17).
   2. God's power comes upon man's weakness.
   3. Mere humans become instruments of the Almighty God and His purposes.
C. Youth have a prominent part in this spiritual awakening.
   1. Note: "Your sons and daughters shall prophesy, your young men will see visions…" (Ac 2:17).
   2. Young people can be filled with the Spirit and proclaim the gospel.
D. The Holy Spirit will be poured out without class distinction.
   1. God will pour out His Spirit "even on my servants."
   2. The Spirit is not just for preachers, but for every believer.
   3. We have all been called as His witnesses (Lk 24:48).
   4. Therefore, we all need God's power (Lk 24:49; Ac 1:8).
E. The Spirit is given without gender distinction.
   1. The Spirit is poured out on "sons and daughters … both men and women" (Ac 2:17-18).
   2. Women were in the upper room (Ac 1:14).
   3. God empowers women for the same reason He empowers men—to preach the gospel (Ac 1:8).

F. It is a universal movement.
      1. The Spirit will be poured out "on *all* people" (Ac 2:17).
      2. The gospel must be preached to all people.
      3. All who receive the gospel can be empowered to preach the gospel to others.

II. **PREPARATION FOR THE OUTPOURING** (Joel 2:12-17)
   (We can do four things to prepare for the Spirit's outpouring:)
   A. First, we must be wholeheartedly repent of our sins (Read: Joel 2:12).
      1. Twice Peter emphasized the need to repent before receiving the Spirit (Ac 2:38; 3:19).
   B. Second, we must come to God with humility and with broken hearts (Read: Joel 2:13. See also Ps 51:17).
      1. Pride and self-will hinders the Spirit's coming.
   C. Third, we must be in unity.
      1. The people are exhorted to come together (Joel 2:15-16).
      2. This is what happened at Pentecost (Ac 2:1).
      3. We must unify around God's mission (Ac 1:8).
   D. Fourth, we must intercede for God's Spirit (Ac 1:14).
      1. The prophet calls on the people to pray (Joel 2:17).
      2. Before Pentecost the people were in prayer (Ac 1:14).

Conclusion and Altar Call
   1. Come, receive the Spirit today.
   2. How?
      a. Ask (Lk 11:9-10,13)
      b. Receive (Mk 11:24)
      c. Speak (Ac 2:4, 17).

[MH]

*Adapted from Melvin L. Hodges, *When the Spirit Comes,* Springfield, MO: Gospel Publishing House, 1972, pp. 3-13.

32. Springs and Streams of Living Water
Two Powerful Works of the Spirit in John's Gospel

Sermon in a Sentence: The Holy Spirit wants to work in and through you, imparting life to you and dispensing life to others.

Sermon Purpose: That sinners may be born again and believers may be empowered by the Holy Spirit

Texts: John 4:10-14; John 7:37-39

Introduction
1. In our texts Jesus used two pictures to describe the work of the Spirit in people's lives:
   a. In John 4, Jesus describes the Spirit as becoming "a spring of water" working "in" a person resulting in "eternal life."
   b. In John 7, Jesus describes the Spirit as becoming "rivers of living water" flowing out "from within" a person giving life to others.
2. The two pictures represent two powerful works of the Spirit in believers' lives:
   a. The Spirit working *in* a person to bring eternal life.
      1) i.e., the new birth.
      2) Jesus spoke of this in John 3:1-7.
   b. The Spirit working *through* a believer's life to dispense life and blessing to others.
      1) The baptism in the Holy Spirit.
      2) Spoken of in John 1:33.
3. Let's look more closely at each of these two essential experiences as presented by John.

I. **THE NEW BIRTH: A SPRING OF LIVING WATER** (Jn 4:10-14)
   A. Our text reveals how the gift is received.
      1. Realize that it comes from God (v. 10 "the gift of God").
      2. Know that it is for everyone (v. 13 "everyone who drinks").
      3. Ask Christ for the gift (v. 10 "you would have asked him").
      4. Drink deeply from the well (v.14 "whoever drinks").
   B. Out text also speaks of the results of receiving the gift.
      1. On receives "eternal life" (v. 14 "welling up to eternal life").
      2. As a result, they "will never thirst again" (v. 13).

II. **THE BAPTISM IN THE HOLY SPIRIT: RIVERS OF LIVING WATER** (Jn 7:37-38)
   A. Jesus tells how the gift is received.

1. Must thirst (v. 37 "If anyone is thirsty").
2. Must come to Jesus and drink (v. 37 "must come to me and drink").
3. Must exercise faith (v. 38 "whoever believes").
B. Then, Jesus tells the result of receiving the gift.
   1. v. 38 "streams of living water will flow from within him".
   2. The believer's life will become a source of life and blessing to others.
   3. The Spirit will empower us.
      a. To be Christ's witnesses (Ac 1:8: 4:8, 31).
      b. To advance God's kingdom and set people free from demonic bondage (Mt 12:28).
      c. To work the works of Christ (Jn 14:12, 16).

Conclusion and Altar Call
1. You ask, how can I receive eternal life?
   a. Repent of your sins.
   b. Put you faith in Christ.
2. Others ask, how can I receive the power of the Holy Spirit?
   a. Ask in faith (Lk 11:9, 13).
   b. Receive by faith (Lk 11:10; Mk 11:24).
   c. Speak in faith (Ac 2:4).

[DRM]

33 Suddenly From Heaven

Sermon in a Sentence: You can be baptized in the Holy Spirit like the believers at Pentecost.
Sermon Purpose: That the listeners be filled and/or refilled with the Holy Spirit according to the biblical pattern of Pentecost.
Text: Acts 2:1-4

Introduction
1. The experience at Pentecost serves as a pattern for us today.
2. You can expect the Holy Spirit to come upon you and fill you just as the He filled the believers on the Day of Pentecost.
3. Just as on the Day of Pentecost there are seven things you can expect to happen when you come to be filled with the Holy Spirit:

I. **YOU CAN EXPECT THE HOLY SPIRIT TO COME UPON YOU SUDDENLY.**
   A. Note how the Spirit came on the Day of Pentecost:
      1. v. 2 "*suddenly* there came a sound from heaven …"
      2. The same thing occurred at Cornelius house (Ac 10:44).
   B. Here is what you can expect to happen as you pray.
      1. You will sense the Spirit's presence coming upon you.
      2. The moment you believe, you will receive the Spirit.

II. **YOU CAN EXPECT THE HOLY SPIRIT TO COME UPON YOU SUPERNATURALLY.**
   A. Look what happened on the Day of Pentecost:
      1. v. 2 there came a sound "from Heaven" (i.e., from God).
      2. The Spirit supernaturally manifested God's presence (as a supernatural sound of wind; as a supernatural fire; and as supernatural tongues).
   B. Being baptized in the Holy Spirit is a supernatural event.
      1. It is a mighty visitation from heaven.
      2. It is a person-to-person encounter with a living God.
      3. It is a dynamic life-changing event.
   C. Expect to feel His mighty presence and power.

III. **YOU CAN EXPECT THE HOLY SPIRIT TO COME UPON YOU POWERFULLY.**
   A. Note that at Pentecost the Holy Spirit did not only come as a wind, He came as a "*mighty rushing* wind" (Ac 2:2).
   B. When the Spirit comes, He comes in power, resulting in …
      1. … a powerful empowering (Ac 1:8).
      2. … powerful inner change (i.e., Peter).

IV. YOU CAN EXPECT THE HOLY SPIRIT TO COME UPON YOU PERSONALLY.
  A. Look how He came on the Day of Pentecost:
   1. v. 3 "there appeared . . . fire *and sat on each of them.*"
   2. Each one had a unique, personal encounter with God.
  B. The Holy Spirit will come upon you as an individual.
   1. He knows your personality, and your needs.
   2. The Holy Spirit fills all types of people and personalities.

V. YOU CAN EXPECT THE HOLY SPIRIT TO COME UPON YOU PERVASIVELY. (Note: "Pervasively" means filling every part.)
  A. When the Holy Spirit comes upon you He will fill your entire being.
   1. He will fill your body, spirit, and soul.
   2. He comes in three ways:
      a. As an invasion from without (He will "come upon").
      b. A total immersion in (He will "baptize" you).
      c. As a permeation within (He will "fill" you).
   3. ILLUS: Like water fills every cell of a sponge.
  B. When you come to be filled expect to be immersed in the presence and power of God.

VI. YOU CAN EXPECT THE HOLY SPIRIT TO COME UPON YOU VERIFIABLY.
  A. At Pentecost "they were all filled...and began to speak in other tongues..." (Ac 2:4).
  B. When He fills you, there will be no doubt.
   1. He will give you an undeniable evidence.
   2. You will speak in tongues as the Spirit enables you.
  C. The same thing happened at Caesarea (Acts 10:45-46).
   1. Tongues settled the question! (vv. 46-47).
  D. When you come to be filled expect speak a new tongue as the Spirit enables you.

VII. YOU CAN EXPECT THE HOLY SPIRIT TO COME UPON YOU PURPOSEFULLY.
  A. They began to speak "... as the Spirit enabled them."
  B. The Spirit came to enable them to speak ...
   1. ... first in tongues,
   2. ... then as Spirit-empowered witnesses (cf. Acts 1:8)
  C. Never forget, the Spirit's purpose in filling you is to empower you as Christ's witness.

Conclusion and Altar Call
  Come now and be filled with the Spirit like the Day of Pentecost.
  [DRM]

34. Times of Refreshing from the Presence of the Lord

Sermon in a Sentence: God wants to give you "times of refreshing from the presence of the Lord" by filling you with His Holy Spirit.
Sermon Purpose: That believers will be baptized in the Holy Spirit.
Text: Acts 3:19

Introduction
1. Our text is found in Peter's second sermon in Acts. (Tell Story.)
2. It is a description of the baptism in the Holy Spirit.
    a. Here Peter describes the baptism in the Spirit as "times of refreshing ...from the presence of the Lord."
    b. These words remind us of Acts 2:38-39.
3. This message will focus on Peter's description.
    a. A close look at this phrase reveals three important truths about the experience of the baptism in the Holy Spirit:

I. **THE BAPTISM IN THE HOLY SPIRIT IS NOT A MAN-MADE EXPERIENCE.**
   A. It does not have its origin in the will or mind of man.
      1. It is not an invention of modern Pentecostalism.
      2. It is an experience from God!
         a. "times of refreshing from the presence of the Lord."
         b. Literally, "from the face of the Lord."
      3. Acts 2:3: "Suddenly there came a sound *from heaven.*"
      4. It's "the promise of the Father" (Ac 1:4).
   B. It is a life-changing encounter with the living God.
      1. In order to properly receive the Holy Spirit, we must have a clear understanding of who He really is.
         a. The Holy Spirit is in fact God!
         b. Therefore, everything that can be said about God can be said about the Holy Spirit. (i.e., God and the Spirit are holy, omnipotent, eternal, etc.)
      2. Therefore, to be filled with the Spirit is to be filled with the very presence and power of God!
         a. A time of refreshing from the presence of the Lord!
         b. Receiving the Spirit turns us into a channel of God's power and love to others (Jn 7:37, Acts 1:8).

II. **THE BAPTISM IN THE HOLY SPIRIT IS NOT A DRY, UNEMOTIONAL EXPERIENCE.**
   A. It is a time of refreshing!
      1. Williams translates it as "times of revival."

  2. The New Living Bible translates the phrase as "a time when your soul will receive strength."
  3. Paul wrote, "He who speaks in a tongue edifies himself" (1Co 14:3-4).
 B. Being filled with the Spirit will bring you into a more intimate relationship with God (Ro 5:5; ref. Ps 42:1, 2).
  1. Various biblical symbols for the Holy Spirit speak of how He refreshes and revives our souls:
   a. He quenches spiritual thirst like cool water (Jn 4:13).
   b. He enters our lives like refreshing rain (Zec 10:1).
   c. He flows through our being like a life-giving river (Jn 7:37; Eze 47:1-12).
   d. He blows into our lives like a cool breeze (Jn 3:8).
  2. Let Him blow into your life today!

III. THE BAPTISM IN THE HOLY SPIRIT IT IS NOT A ONE-TIME-ONLY EXPERIENCE.
 A. Note that the word "times" is plural, indicating multiple experiences.
 B. Some make the mistake of thinking that one experience with the Spirit is enough.
  1. No matter how powerful or life-changing your experience with the Spirit was, one experience is not enough.
 C. In the New Testament we see repeated fillings:
  1. Peter: (Ac 2:4 then 4:8 the 4:31).
  2. Ephesians: (Ac 9:6 then Eph 5:18)
  3. The literal translation of Luke 11:9-10 is "Keep on asking … keep on seeking … keep on knocking"
  4. We must keep seeking the Lord for repeated fillings with the Spirit.

Conclusion and Altar Call
 1. You ask, "How can I receive the Holy Spirit today?
 2. Our text tells us: "Repent and return, so that your sins may be wiped away, in order that times of refreshing may come …"
 3. Do this:
  a) Return to the Lord
  b) Repent of your sins
  c) Ask Him to fill you
  d) Believe His promise.
 4. Come now and be filled.

[DRM]

35. The Two Fillings of Pentecost

Sermon in a Sentence: We can experience the presence of the Spirit in our services and the power of the Spirit in our lives.

Sermon Purpose: To encourage believers to open their hearts to the presence of the Spirit and to be personally baptized in the Holy Spirit.

Text: Acts 2:1-4

Introduction
1. Tell the story of the outpouring of the Spirit at Pentecost.
2. On the Day of Pentecost there were actually two fillings with the Holy Spirit.
    a. v. 2 The Spirit "filled the whole house."
    b. v. 4 "they were all filled" with the Holy Spirit.
3. God wants to do the same for us today.

I. **GOD WANTS TO FILL THIS PLACE** (v. 2).
   A. In the Bible the Spirit often filled certain places.
      1. In the Old Testament God's presence filled the Temple (2 Ch 5:13).
      2. In the book of Acts the Spirit often filled a place and manifested His powerful presence.
         a. At Pentecost (Ac 2:1-4).
         b. Again in Jerusalem (Ac 4:31).
      3. God wants to fill this place today.
   B. The Spirit comes to fill a place for certain purposes:
      1. To make His presence known.
      2. To convict the sinner of his sin.
      3. To expose and defeat the powers of Satan.
      4. To meet the needs of His people.
      5. To empower His church to preach the gospel.
   C. How may we experience God's presence?
      1. We must pray.
      2. We must open our lives to the Spirit.
      3. We must welcome Him when He comes.
   D. God wants to fill this place today.

II. **GOD WANTS TO FILL HIS PEOPLE** (v. 4).
   A. God's chief interest is people rather than places.
      1. The main filling at Pentecost was the people.
      2. God's will is to fill every believer with the Holy Spirit.
         a. v. 4 "they were *all* filled".
         b. "The promise is for ... *all*" (Ac 2:38-39).
   B. The Spirit fills God's people for certain purposes:

      1. To empower them for witness.
      2. To arm them for spiritual warfare.
      3. To enable them to live holy lives.
  C. When God fills His people …
      1. … they become strong.
      2. … they become bold.

III. GOD WANTS TO FILL AND RE-FILL YOU TODAY.
  A. He has a plan for your life.
  B. God has promised you power to fulfill that plan (Ac 1:8).
  C. Be filled with the Holy Spirit today!
      1. Ask in faith (Lk 11:9,13).
      2. Receive by faith (Lk 11:10; Mk 11:24).
      3. Speak in faith (Ac 2:4; Jn 7:37-38).

Conclusion and Altar Call
Come now to be filled with the Holy Spirit.

[DRM]

36. What Does It Mean To Be Filled With The Holy Spirit?

Sermon in a Sentence: We need to open our minds and hearts to receive the Holy Spirit today.
Sermon Purpose: That believers will open their hearts and be filled with the Spirit.
Text: John 7:37-39

Introduction
1. Have you ever tried to feed a baby who doesn't want to be fed? The baby will refuse to eat!
2. Similarly, the Holy Spirit does not force Himself on us to "fill" us.
3. Just as a baby has desire for food, so we must desire the presence of the Holy Spirit in our lives.
4. This message will answer three important questions about receiving the Holy Spirit:

I. WHAT THINGS DO WE NEED TO BE BAPTIZED IN THE HOLY SPIRIT?
A. We need to have an *open mind* concerning the experience.
   1. We need to believe that this is a biblical, valid experience for today!
B. We need to *understand the purpose* of the experience.
   1. It's purpose is empowerment to witness (Ac 1:8).
      a. After Jesus' resurrection the disciples wanted immediately to go and preach the gospel.
      b. But Jesus knew that they weren't yet ready.
      c. He said, "Before you fulfill your call, you need to be filled with the Spirit" (Lk 24:46-49; Ac 1:4-8)
   2. Peter preached that all believers need the "gift of the Holy Spirit" (Ac 2:38-39).
   3. Paul told twelve men in Ephesus that they needed to receive the Holy Spirit (Ac 19:1-7).
C. We need to *believe* that Christ wants to fill us with the Spirit.

II. WHY DO WE NEED TO BE FILLED WITH THE HOLY SPIRIT?
A. We need to be filled for the sake of *spiritual priorities*.
   1. Jesus taught that the Holy Spirit was sent to testify about Him (Jn 15:26).
   2. The believer's priority is to praise Jesus and proclaim Him to the lost (Ac 4:8-12).
B. We need to be filled for the sake of *spiritual purity*.
   1. When the Holy Spirit is at work in us, we are more aware of sin, righteousness, and judgment (Jn 16:8-11).

        2. Therefore, we will be more pure.
    C. We need to be filled for the sake of *spiritual power*.
        1. We all need the strength, courage, and boldness that the Spirit provides (Ac 4:13, 18-20, 31).

III HOW CAN WE BE FILLED WITH THE SPIRIT TODAY?
    A. We must have *willing spirits*.
        1. It's not enough just to believe; we must also desire.
        2. Desire follows our recognition of need.
            a. Like the woman with an issue of blood (Mk 5:28).
            b. Like blind Bartimeaus (Mk 10:46-48).
        3. When we recognize how truly weak we are in ourselves, we will earnestly desire to be filled with the Holy Spirit.
        4. God fills those who crave the Spirit (Mt 5:6).
    B. We must have *yielded bodies.*
        1. John 7:37-39 teaches that we must be thirsty and yielded. (Thirsty: "Is anyone thirsty?" Yielded: "Whoever believes …"
        2. We must yield our entire beings to God (Ro 6:13).
            a. Including our tongues.
            b. We provide the instruments, the Spirit provides the enablement (Ac 2:4).
            c. The disciples speaking in tongues was the result of their being filled with the Holy Spirit, not the purpose.
            d. The purpose was to glorify Jesus and become an effective witness (Ac 1:8).

Conclusion and Altar Call
    1. Desire to be Christ's witness.
    2. Open your life to the Spirit's working.
    3. Come now to be filled with the Spirit.

[DC]

37. You Can Experience the True Baptism in the Holy Spirit

Sermon in a Sentence: You can experience the true baptism in the Holy Spirit today.
Sermon Purpose: To see believers truly baptized in the Holy Spirit.
Text: Acts 2:1-4

Introduction
1. Today many are confused about the baptism in the Holy Spirit.
2. Many claim to have been filled who have not really been filled.
3. We need a clear word on the experience.
4. Our text gives us three truths concerning a true baptism in the Holy Spirit.

I. **THE TRUE BAPTISM IN THE HOLY SPIRIT IS CLOSELY ASSOCIATED WITH GOD'S HARVEST** (Ac 2:1).
   A. Historically Pentecost was a Jewish harvest festival (Lev 23:11-16; Dt 16:9-10).
      1. God providentially chose to send the Holy Spirit during this harvest festival.
      2. Pentecost thus symbolizes the beginning of God's worldwide harvest of souls.
   B. The power of Pentecost is to promote the growth of the church worldwide (Ac 1:8).

II. **THE TRUE BAPTISM IN THE HOLY SPIRIT IS FOR BORN AGAIN BELIEVERS—GOD'S NEW TEMPLE** (Ac 2:2-3).
   A. In the Old Testament wind and fire symbolized God's presence.
      1. The sound of wind reminded those present that God was about to do something.
      2. The fire signified God's acceptance of the church as God's new temple (2Ch 7:1-3; 1Co 3:16; Eph 2:21-22).
      3. The individual flames indicated that each believer was a temple of the Holy Spirit (1Co 6:19).
   B. As a living temple of the Holy Spirit, every true believer can be empowered by the Holy Spirit. (As a living temple ...)
      1. Every believer should be a place of faith, worship, sacrifice, thanksgiving, witness, and offering.
      2. Every true believer in Christ is ready to be baptized in and empowered by the Holy Spirit.
      3. Just as an artist can take a blank piece of paper and turn it into a thing of great value, God can take a sinful life,

wash it in the blood of Jesus, fill it with His Spirit, and make it a blessing to the whole world.

III. THE TRUE BAPTISM IN THE HOLY SPIRIT CAN BE YOURS TODAY (Ac 2:4).
  A. At Pentecost *all* were baptized in the Holy Spirit.
  1. God's plan for believers today is for all to be filled.
  2. This includes you.
  B. The Bible uses a number of terms to describe this experience:
  1. Such as filling, pouring out, falling on, receiving, baptizing.
  2. These terms describe a relational experience with the Holy Spirit.
  C. When you are filled with the Spirit you will speak in tongues as the Spirit enables.
  1. At Pentecost they spoke as the Spirit gave the words (Ac 2:4).
  2. This is the only repeated sign of Spirit baptism in the book of Acts (Ac 2:4; 10:45; 19:6).
  3. The words will not come from your mind, but from your spirit (1Co 14:2).
  D. You will become a powerful witness for Christ (Ac 1:8).
  E. Many other results will follow (such as a closer relationship with God, power over demons, spiritual gifts, etc.).

Conclusion and Altar Call
Come and experience the true baptism in the Holy Spirit today.

[JWL]

Section 2

Spirit-Empowered Missions and Ministry

38. Advancing the Kingdom of God

Sermon in a Sentence: Jesus advanced the kingdom of God by the power of the Holy Spirit, and we should do the same when we are filled with the Holy Spirit.

Sermon Purpose: To see people empowered by the Holy Spirit to advance the kingdom of God.

Text: Matthew 12:22-28, Acts 1:3-5, 8

Introduction
1. A cosmic war is taking place between the kingdom of God and the kingdom of Satan (Eph 6:12).
2. The kingdom of God is powerfully advancing in spite of those who try to stop it (Mt 11:12 NIV).
3. Jesus declared that the kingdom of Satan will not withstand the advance of the kingdom of God through the church (Mt 16:18).
4. In this message we will answer the question, "How does the kingdom of God advance?"

I. **JESUS ADVANCED THE KINGDOM OF GOD IN THE POWER OF THE HOLY SPIRIT** (Mt 12:22-28).
   A. Jesus often healed and delivered people who were under the power of demonic spirits.
      1. Jesus' power over demons signified that the kingdom of God was triumphing over the kingdom of Satan.
   B. Our text in Matthew is a significant example of Jesus advancing the kingdom of God.
      1. In this text Jesus made a declaration that revealed two important truths:
   C. First, Jesus revealed that the Holy Spirit was the source of His power (v.28a).
      1. "I drive out demons *by the Spirit of God.*"
      2. Through the incarnation Jesus became a man.
      3. The Holy Spirit came upon Jesus as a man and empowered Him for ministry (Lk 3:21-22; 4:1, 14-21).
      4. Everything Jesus did in ministry He did by the power of the Holy Spirit (Ac 10:38).
      5. This is an important truth because Jesus is the ultimate example of how we should serve God.
   D. Second, Jesus revealed that the Kingdom of God advances in the power of the Holy Spirit.
      1. "If I drive out demons *by the Spirit of God* then *the kingdom of God has come upon you.*"
      2. It is humanly impossible to overcome the power of Satan.

      3. Satan, however, cannot withstand the advance of the kingdom of God in the power of the Holy Spirit.

II. LIKE JESUS, WE TOO CAN ADVANCE THE KINGDOM OF GOD IN THE POWER OF THE HOLY SPIRIT (Ac 1:3-5, 8).
  A. Jesus promised His disciples—and us—the same power of the Holy Spirit that He used to advance the Kingdom of God.
    1. After the resurrection, Jesus continued to teach His disciples about the kingdom of God (Ac 1:3).
    2. He emphasized that they would advance the kingdom of God through the power of the Holy Spirit (vv. 4-5, 8).
      a. The Holy Spirit is so important that Jesus instructed them to wait until they had received Him (v. 4).
      b. He explained that they would receive the power of the Holy Spirit by being *baptized* in the Spirit (v. 5,8).
      c. On the Day of Pentecost the Holy Spirit came upon them and they were filled with His presence and power just as Jesus had promised (Ac 2:1-4).
      d. The rest of the book of Acts shows how the early church advanced the kingdom of God in the power of the Holy Spirit.
  B. The promise of the Holy Spirit is for us today just as it was for the early disciples (Ac 2:38-39).
    1. We are still at war against demonic powers.
    2. Many are oppressed and in bondage to sin and the power of Satan.
    3. The world's only hope is a church that is empowered by the Spirit and able to advance against Satan.
  C. Today we must believe Christ's promise and ask Him to fill us with the Spirit's power to advance the kingdom of God.
    1. When we are filled with the Spirit, we can powerfully proclaim the gospel and see the kingdom of God come in power.
    2. If we will seek to be filled with the Spirit, God will work through us to set captives free and advance His kingdom just as He did through Jesus (Jn 14:12, 16-17).

Conclusion and Altar Call
  1. Come in faith and commit yourself to advancing the kingdom of God.
  2. If we ask God, He will fill us with the power of His Spirit and enable us to advance His kingdom (Lk 11:9, 13).

[MT]

39. All of the Lord's People Prophets

Sermon in a Sentence: God wants you to become His Spirit-empowered witness.

Sermon Purpose: That every believer will be filled with the Spirit and realize that, as a result, he or she is to become Christ's prophetic voice declaring the gospel to the lost in the power of the Holy Spirit.

Text: Numbers 11:26-29

Introduction
1. In these last days God is raising up an army of Spirit-empowered prophets to declare the message of Christ to the nations.
2. It has always been God's plan that His people be a community of Spirit-anointed prophets (i.e., Spirit-empowered witnesses.)
3. Let's look into the Bible and discover God's plan:

I. MOSES WISHED FOR IT.
   A. Tell the story of Moses and the seventy elders (Nu 11:16-30).
   B. Moses wished that all of the Lord's People would be Spirit-anointed prophets (Nu 11:28-29).
   C. Why did Moses wish this?
      1. So they could be empowered to help him in the work.
      2. Today Jesus enlists our help in preaching the gospel to the nations.
      3. To do this we must be filled with the Spirit.

II. JOEL CONFIRMED IT.
   A. What Moses wished for Joel confirmed
      1. Read Joel 2:28-29.
      2. The prophet is saying that day would certainly come when God would make all of His people prophets.
      3. He also revealed that the promise would be fulfilled preceding a time of great spiritual harvest (Joel 2:23-24).
   B. We are living in that time of spiritual harvest.

III. PETER DECLARED IT.
   A. Joel's prophecy was first fulfilled on the Day of Pentecost.
      1. Tell the story of Pentecost (Ac 2:1-13).
   B. Peter declared that the time had arrive that all of God's people would be prophets (Ac 2:14-17).
      1. Peter said that "this is that" (v. 16, KJV).

      2. He was saying that *this* experience of being filled with the Spirit and speaking in Gentile tongues is the fulfillment of *that* which Joel prophesied.
- C. From this we learn three powerful truths:
  1. This outpouring would take place in the Last Days (Ac 2:17).
  2. Its purpose would be empowerment for mission (Ac 1:8).
  3. It is for all of God's people—i.e., sons and daughters, young and old, slave and free (Ac 2:17).

IV. WE CAN EXPERIENCE IT.
- A. God intends for His church to be a Spirit-empowered witnessing community.
- B. You can become one of God's last-days prophets by being filled with the Spirit and by committing yourself to fulfilling the Great Commission of Christ.
- C. The promise is for you today (Ac 2:38-39).

Conclusion and Altar Call
1. Come, commit yourself to fulfilling God's mission.
2. You will be filled with the Spirit and empowered for the mission.

[DRM]

40. The Anointing that Breaks the Yoke

Sermon in a Sentence: We must be anointed by the Spirit so that we may break the yokes that bind people.

Sermon Purpose: That believers might be baptized in the Holy Spirit and anointed by the Spirit to set people free from their bondages.

Text: Isaiah 10:27 (KJV)

I. **THE JUDGES BROKE THE YOKE BECAUSE OF THE ANOINTING.**
   A. They broke political bondages through the power of the Holy Spirit.
   B. Five examples in the Judges:
      1. Othniel (Jdg 3:10)
      2. Deborah (Jdg 4:4)
      3. Gideon (Jdg 6:14, 34)
      4. Jephthah (Jdg 11:29)
      5. Samson
         a. The Spirit stirred him (Jdg 13:25).
         b. The Spirit came upon him (Jdg 14:14).

II. **JESUS BROKE THE YOKE BECAUSE OF THE ANOINTING.**
   A. Jesus declared that through the Spirit He would break spiritual, physical, and emotional bondages (Lk 4:17-18).
   B. Peter summarized Jesus' Spirit-anointed ministry (Ac 10:38).

III. **THE DISCIPLES BROKE THE YOKE BECAUSE OF THE ANOINTING.**
   A. Jesus promised to give to His followers the same anointing that was upon Him (Lk 24:49; Ac 1:4-5; 1:8).
   B. He fulfilled that promise at Pentecost (Ac 2:1-4).
   C. Once they had received the Spirit, the disciples went out and ministered in the power and anointing of the Holy Spirit.
      1. For example: Peter and John's anointed ministry at the Beautiful Gate (Ac 3:1-10).

IV. **TODAY WE, TOO, HAVE BEEN CALLED TO BREAK YOKES BECAUSE OF THE ANOINTING.**
   A. Today people are bound by many things.
      1. Bound by sin.
      2. Bound by occultism.
      3. Bound by Islam.
   B. We must be anointed by the Spirit if we are going to be used by God to break these yokes.

- C. How can we have this anointing?
  1. We must submit ourselves to the "Anointer" (Jesus).
  2. We must be in unity.
     a. Our unity is a unity of purpose … of promotion … of determination.
     b. Ps. 133:1-3. (Note how this unity results in anointing which results in blessing.)
  3. We must be available to Jesus to allow Him to anoint us.

Conclusion and Altar Call
Come to receive the anointing by being baptized in the Holy Spirit.

[JI]

* These notes are transcribed from a message preached by Dr. Ikoni at the AAGA General Assembly in Honey Dew, South Africa, 9-12 March 2009.

41. Competent Ministers of the Spirit

Sermon in a Sentence: We can all be competent ministers of the Spirit.

Sermon Purpose: That believers will be filled with the Spirit and commit themselves to becoming competent ministers of the Spirit.

Text: 2 Corinthians 3:5-6

Introduction
1. We are called to be competent ministers of the Spirit.
2. To be a competent minister of the Spirit means at least four things:

I. IT MEANS THAT THE MINISTER HIMSELF (OR HERSELF) HAS BEEN FILLED WITH THE SPIRIT AND MAINTAINS A DAILY WALK IN THE SPIRIT.
  A. The baptism in the Holy Spirit is the basic requirement for spiritual ministry (Lk 24:49; Ac 1:1-8).
  B. The minister must also maintain a daily walk in the Spirit (Gal 5:16, 25).
   1. Remaining full of the Spirit must be the our chief goal.
   2. This is done through prayer, sensitivity to the Spirit, obedience, and holiness of life.

II. IT MEANS THAT THE MINISTER IS ABLE TO EFFECTIVELY PROCLAIM THE WORD IN THE POWER OF THE HOLY SPIRIT.
  A. The minister's primary responsibility is to preach Christ in the power of the Holy Spirit (Mk 16:15-16; Ac 1:8).
  B. This was the apostolic model (Ac 4:8-12).

III. IT MEANS THAT THE MINISTER IS ABLE TO LEAD OTHERS INTO THE FULNESS OF THE SPIRIT.
  A. This was a primary goal of Jesus and the apostles:
   1. Jesus' first act after His resurrection (Jn 20:21-22).
   2. Jesus' last command (Ac 1:1-8).
   3. The apostles' first concern for Samaria (Ac 8:17-18).
   4. Paul's first concern in Ephesus (Ac 19:1-2).
  B. This must be one of our chief goals in ministry.

IV. IT MEANS THAT THE MINISTER IS ABLE TO MINISTER IN THE GIFTS OF THE HOLY SPIRIT AND TEACH OTHERS TO DO THE SAME.
  A. Jesus promised to give us power (Ac 1:8).

      1. This power is primarily manifested in spiritual gifts.
- B. Spiritual gifts will…
  1. … equip us to edify the church.
  2. …enable us to effectively spread the gospel.
  3. … arm us for spiritual warfare.
- C. We must be competent ministers of these spiritual gifts.
- D. We must be able to teach others how to minister spiritual gifts.

Conclusion and Altar Call

I close with two important questions:
1. How do we get to be competent ministers of the Spirit?
   a. We are qualified by the Spirit of God.
   b. Remember, "we are "not competent in ourselves" (2 Co 3:5).
   c. But, "our competence comes from God."
2. What must we do about these things now?
   a. Decide
   b. Commit
   c. Be filled/re-filled with the Spirit.

[DRM]

42 Dunamis–Martus

Sermon in a Sentence: We must all be filled with God's *dunamis* (power) in order to be His *martus* (witnesses) to the nations.

Sermon Purpose: That believers understand their role as witnesses for Christ and then receive the Spirit's power to carry out that role.

Text: Acts 1:8

Introduction
1. Our text contains the final words of Jesus before His ascension into heaven (Acts 1:8).
   a. These words clearly define the mission of the church.
   b. They also reveal the church's evangelistic pattern: "Receive power (then) be His witnesses."
   c. The verse thus contains two key words, "power" and "witness."
   d. The Greek for these two words is *dunamis* and *martus*.
2. In this message we will look closely at these two Greek words, and we will draw some implications from what we find.

I. *DUNAMIS* (POWER)
A. Note that we are talking here about the *dunamis* of God.
   1. This *dunamis* is God's possession alone to give.
   2. It belongs to Him, therefore, only He can give it away.
B. The word *dunamis* is used 120 times in the Greek NT.
   1. 77 times it is translated "power."
   2. It is also translated as "mighty works," "strength," "miracles," and "virtue."
C. Broadly defined, the word *dunamis* means strength, power, or ability.
   1. It is inherent power or "power within."
   2. It is power residing within by virtue of its nature.
   3. It includes miracle-working power, moral power, money power, and military power.
D. This power is not limited by what we feel or don't feel, by what we do or don't do.
   1. It is the all-encompassing *dunamis* of God.
   2. it is manifested in powerful witness, including signs, wonders, moral power, and excellence of soul.
   3. It is the power which He desires to give us!
E. It is the *dunamis* of God at work among the nations of the world, at work on the continent of Africa, at work across ethnic and language barriers, at work in our families, at work right here in this room, at work in your life today.

II *MARTUS* (WITNESS)
   A. The word *martus* is used 34 times in the Greek NT.
      1. 29 times it is translated "witness."
      2. It is also translated "martyr" and "record."
      3. A witness gives testimony through words, through actions, and through sacrifice.
   B. There are several ways of understanding this word:
      1. For example, a witness in a courtroom.
      2. Or, someone who watches an event (a spectator).
      3. Or, one who gives his life for a cause (a martyr).
      4. *Martus* certainly includes preaching and verbal witness; however, it is much more.
   C. Let's look at two *martus* in the book of Acts:
      1. Steven was a witness in multiple ways.
         a. He was a man full of faith and the Holy Spirit (6:5).
         b. He did great wonders among the people (6:8).
         c. He spoke with power (6:10).
         d. He showed moral courage in death (7:56-60).
      2. Paul (Saul of Tarsus) presents a different, but equally significant, paradigm of witness.
         a. He consented to the death of Stephen (Ac 8:1).
         b. Stephen's witness contributed to his conversion.
         c. Throughout his ministry Paul witnessed through powerful preaching, signs and wonders, moral character, etc.
         d. Like Stephen, Saul gave his life, through a life lived "dead to self" and "alive to Christ."
   D. So, the early church was emboldened by the *dunamis* of God and committed to the *martus* of Christ.
      1. As a result the gospel spread through Jerusalem, Judea and Samaria, to the "uttermost" of that era.

Conclusion and Altar Call
   1. Come now and commit yourself to Christ as His *martus*.
   2. And receive His *dunamis* to proclaim His message to all people until He returns from heaven.

[DT]

43. Empowered for the Last Days

Sermon in a Sentence: We must be empowered by the Holy Spirit in order to fulfill our mission for the last days.

Sermon Purpose: To see believers baptized in the Holy Spirit so that they may participate in God's last-days harvest.

Text: Acts 2:17

Introduction
1. The final days in preparation for any event are always a time of increased and urgent activity.
   a. For example, preparation for a wedding.
2. Our text speaks of the "Last Days," a time of increased and urgent activity in the spiritual realm.
3. Based on our text, we will ask and answer three questions about the Last Days:

I. WHAT IS MEANT BY THE PHRASE "THE LAST DAYS?"
   A. The ancient Jews saw the Last Days as a time of Messianic blessing.
      1. A time when God will bring judgment on the ungodly.
      2. And vindication to His people.
   B. In the New Testament we have a fuller revelation of the Last Days.
      1. Peter identified the Last Days as a time of the pouring out of God's Spirit on all mankind (see text).
      2. It encompasses the entire church age.
         a. It began with the first coming of Jesus in the power of the Spirit and the outpouring of the Spirit on the Day of Pentecost.
         b. It extends until the second coming of Christ.
      3. We are living in the Last Days.
         a. We are a "Last Days People."
         b. We are living "between the times." (that is, the time of Jesus' first and second comings).
         c. We must, therefore, live with a sense of expectation and urgency (Ac 1:10-11).

II. WHAT ARE SOME OF THE DOMINANT CHARACTERISTICS OF THE LAST DAYS?
   (There are many. We will speak of four:)
   A. A time of "finishing up" of God's plan for the nations (Ac 3:19-21).
   B. A time of a world-wide outpouring of the Spirit (that is., "on all mankind").

C. A time when the gospel will be preached in power to all nations (Mt 24:14; Ac 1:8; 2:21).
   D. A time of great prophetic activity and a powerful demonstration of God's power against the kingdom of Satan (Ac 2:14-18; cf. Mt 12:28).

III. WHAT ARE SOME IMPLICATIONS OF THESE TRUTHS ON US TODAY AS PENTECOSTAL PEOPLE?
   A. We must each realize that we have been called and empowered to participate in God's plan for the nations.
   B. As God's "Last Days People" we must sense the urgency of our task. (Jn 9:4).
   C. We must each be personally empowered by the Spirit to carry out our ministries (Lk 24:49; Ac 1:4-5).

Conclusion and Altar Call
   1. You ask, "How can I participate in God's great last day's mission?"
      a. Understand that you are one of God's "Last Days People."
      b. Be filled with the Spirit today.
   2. What must one do to be filled with the Spirit?
      a. Ask in faith (Lk 11:9-13).
      b. Receive by faith (Mk 11:24).
      c. Speak in faith (Ac 2:4).

[DRM]

44. The Empowering of the Spirit and the Great Commission

Sermon in a Sentence: We need to be empowered by the Spirit to complete the Great Commission.

Sermon Purpose: That believers be filled with the Spirit in anticipation of participating in fulfilling the Great Commission.

Text: Acts 1:4-8

Introduction
1. In our text Jesus described the baptism in the Holy Spirit as an empowering experience given to complete the Great Commission.
2. The question arises, "Exactly how does the empowering of the Spirit help us in the work evangelism and missions?"
3. The experience helps in at least six important ways:

I. WITH THE EMPOWERING OF THE SPIRIT COMES MOTIVATION TO PROCLAIM CHRIST TO THE LOST.
A. This is what happened to the disciples at Pentecost and after
   1. Example: Peter (Ac 2:14ff).
   2. Believers after Pentecost: (Ac 2:47).
   3. Peter's explanation: (Ac 11:12).
B. This is why we each need to be filled with the Spirit.

II. WITH THE EMPOWERING OF THE SPIRIT COMES POWER TO CHALLENGE AND DEFEAT DEMONIC POWERS.
A. The proclamation of the gospel is being strongly opposed by Satan and his demons (2Co 4:4).
B. We can only overcome these legions of hell through the power of the Spirit (Mt 12:28).

III. WITH THE EMPOWERING OF THE SPIRIT COMES ENABLEMENT TO PREACH WITH GREATER POWER AND EFFECTIVENESS.
A. After Pentecost the disciples preached with great power and effectiveness:
   1. Example: Peter after Pentecost: (Ac 2:41).
   2. Example: Later in Jerusalem: (Ac 4:31-33).
B. God will empower us to do the same.

IV. WITH THE EMPOWERING OF THE SPIRIT COMES BOLDNESS TO PREACH CHRIST, EVEN IN THE FACE OF GREAT DANGER.
A. Proclaiming Christ can often be a dangerous business:

        1. Example: Peter in Jerusalem (Ac 12:1-5).
        2. Example: Paul in Galatia (Ac 14:19-20).
    B. The Spirit will give us boldness in the face of such danger.

V. **WITH THE EMPOWERING OF THE SPIRIT COMES THE EXPECTATION OF DIVINE GUIDANCE.**
    A. The Spirit often guided the New Testament missionaries:
        1. Example: The Spirit guided Philip (Ac 8:29-31).
        2. Example: The Spirit guided Paul (Ac 16:6-9).
    B. The Spirit will guide us today.

VI. **WITH THE EMPOWERING OF THE SPIRIT COMES GREAT CONFIDENCE THAT SOULS WILL BE SAVED AND CHURCHES ESTABLISHED.**
    A. With the baptism in the Holy Spirit comes confidence that God will give success (Lk 5:10).
    B. This confidence will help to encourage us in the work.
        1. Example: Paul (Ac 18:10-11).
    C. With all of these benefits accruing, it is no wonder that Jesus has commanded us to be filled with the Spirit.

Conclusion and Altar Call
  1. Come now to be filled!
  2. How?
      a. Ask in faith (Lk 11:9, 13).
      b. Receive by faith (Lk 11:10; Mk 11:24).
      c. Speak in faith (Ac 2:4, 14; Jn 7:38).

[DRM]

45. God Has Chosen the Weak

Sermon in a Sentence: God often chooses those people and churches who are weak in the world's eyes and empowers them to do great works.

Sermon Purpose: That believers realize that God can use them—if they will be filled with the Spirit and commit themselves to His purposes, and that they will be filled with the Spirit and empowered for the work.

Text: 1 Corinthians 1:26-29

Introduction
1. We often think that God can only use those who have money, power, or special talents.
2. Our text, however, reveals that the truth is often just the opposite.
   a. God often uses those people and things that are weak and insignificant in the world's eyes to accomplish His purposes.
   b. This means that, if you will commit yourself to God's will and be filled with the Spirit, you can be mightily used by God.
3. Let's look more closely at how this works.

I. WE HAVE A TENDENCY TO FOCUS ON OUR WEAKNESSES.
A. This is true for us individually.
   1. We feel inadequate.
   2. As a result, we withdraw from ministry.
B. This is also true for us corporately:
   1. We see our church as weak and insignificant.
   2. Therefore, we fail to move out in ministry to our communities.
C. It is often true for us as Africans:
   1. We sometimes see Africa as poor and powerless.
   2. Therefore, we choose to leave the work of missions to others.

II. WE SHOULD REMEMBER THAT GOD HAS CHOSEN THE WEAK TO ACCOMPLISH HIS WILL.
A. Paul revealed an amazing truth: "God chose the weak things of the world to shame the strong" (1Co 1:27).
B. The Bible is full of examples of this divine principle:
   1. From among the great world empires, God chose the small nation of Israel to be His representatives to the world (Dt 7:6-10).

         2. God chose, David, the least of Jesse's sons, to become king of Israel (1Sa 16:11-13).
         3. Jesus chose common men to be His disciples.
    C. So, if you consider yourself weak and insignificant, rejoice!
         1. Because God has chosen you ... and He wants to anoint and use you.
         2. What's more, God has chosen this church ... and He wants to empower us to reach our communities.
         3. Not only this but, God has chosen Africa ... and He will send His Spirit upon the church of Africa so that it may become a light to the nations.

III. WE SHOULD REJOICE THAT GOD HAS PROMISED US HIS POWER.
   A. That promise is found in Acts 1:8
   B. Why does God choose to use the weak?
         1. Because the weak are available to be used.
         2. So that He might receive the glory (1Co 12:9).
   C. How does God use the weak?
         1. By giving them His Name (Jn 14:13; Ac 3:6).
         2. By empowering them with His Spirit (Ac 1:8).
         3. By sending them out, and accompanying them in the work (Mt 28:18-20).
         4. By supplying their needs (Php 4:19).
         5. By confirming His word with signs following (Mk 16:17-18; Ac 4:33).

Conclusion and Altar Call
   1. God wants to use you in ways you never dreamed possible.
   2. You must commit yourself to His purposes and be filled with His Spirit.
   3. Come now.

[DRM]

46. The God of Every Situation

Sermon in a Sentence: God will empower us to carry out the mission of God even in times of severe opposition.

Sermon Purpose: That believers will be filled with the Spirit and prepared to proclaim the gospel in the midst of persecution.

Text: Acts 4:23-31; 5:17-20, 29

Introduction
1. As God's missionary people we will be required to go many places to proclaim the gospel and plant churches.
2. Like the apostles and evangelists in the book of Acts, we can expect to meet with opposition.
3. From our Scripture readings we can learn three things about how God helps us during times of opposition:

I. WE MUST UNDERSTAND THE REALITY OF OPPOSITION.
A. A true understanding of the power of the Holy Spirit will send us out to preach the gospel.
B. As we go we can expect to meet with satanic opposition.
  1. In our texts the apostles experienced opposition (Ac 4:18-21; 5:27-28, v.33).
  2. Jesus, Himself, was opposed by Satan.
  3. We, too, can expect satanic opposition.
C. Opposition will come from many directions, yet it will have one source.
  1. It my come from religious leaders, from political leaders, from family members, and from other directions.
  2. The one source, however, is Satan (Eph 6:12).
D. We must preach the gospel in spite of satanic opposition.
  1. Opposition did not stop Jesus from preaching.
  2. Opposition did not stop the apostles from preaching.
  3. Opposition must not stop us from preaching.
  4. The angel's exhortation: "Go ... stand ... speak" (Ac 5:20)

II. WE MUST PRAY DURING OUR TIMES OF OPPOSITION.
A. When opposition comes we have choices:
  1. We can give up and run away.
  2. Or we can pray!
B. In the book of Acts the church prayed during its times of persecution and opposition (Ac 4:23-30).
C. What did the believers pray for in this prayer (Ac 4:23-30)?
  1. They did not pray for deliverance.
  2. They prayed according to the Scriptures (Ac 4:25-26).
  3. They prayed for God's will to be done.

      4. They prayed for God to manifest His power.
      5. They prayed for boldness to preach the gospel.
  D. God powerfully answered their prayer (Ac 4:31).
      1. He manifested His presence.
      2. He filled them all with His Spirit.
      3. They preached the word of Christ with boldness (Ac 4: 31-33; 5:29-32).
      4. God will do the same for us—if we will pray!

III. WE MUST EXPERIENCE GOD'S POWER IN THE MIDST OF OPPOSITION. (Read: Ac 4:31)

  A. We must understand that God does not run away during our times of opposition.
      1. He did not desert the apostles, but filled them with His Spirit, His power, and His boldness to preach the gospel in spite of danger.
      2. He will do the same for us.
      3. Sometimes God delivers us from the situation, at other times He gives us courage to endure persecution and to keep preaching the gospel (Heb 11:32-38).
  B. We experience God's power by being filled and re-filled with the Holy Spirit.
      1. This is what happened to the apostles (Ac 4:31; 5:29-32)
      2. We must be filled with the Spirit and we must ensure that our members are filled with the Spirit.
  C. You can receive this power today by being filled or re-filled with the Spirit.

Conclusion and Altar Call

1. Come now and be filled with the Spirit.
2. How can we be filled today?
   a. Ask in faith (Lk 11:9).
   b. Receive by faith (Lk 11:10, 13; Mk 11:24).
   c. Speak in faith (Ac 2:4; Jn 7:38).

[EL]

47. The Great Commission and the Baptism in the Holy Spirit

Sermon in a Sentence: We must each be filled with the Spirit so that we can effectively obey Jesus' command to preach the gospel to all nations and people.

Sermon Purpose: That believers might be filled with the Spirit and commit themselves to obeying the Great Commission.

Texts: Matthew 28:18-20; Mark 16:15-16; Luke 24:46-49; John 20: 21-22; Acts 1:4-8

Introduction
1. During the forty days between Jesus' resurrection and His ascension He repeated the Great Commission five times:
   a. We have just read those instances.
   b. Each time, He connected the fulfilling of that Great Commission with the power and presence of the Holy Spirit.
2. Let's look at each of these instances, and then let's draw some powerful conclusions from what we learn:

I. LET'S LOOK AT EACH OF JESUS' POST-RESURRECTION GREAT COMMISSIONS.
   A. In chronological order:
      1. The night of His resurrection (Jn 20:21).
      2. Sometime later in Galilee (Mt 28:18-20).
      3. On another occasion, when He appeared to the eleven as they were eating (Mk 16:15-16).
      4. Just before His ascension (Lk 24:46-48; Ac 1:8b).
   B. Notice these significant facts about these statements:
      1. The Great Commission was Jesus' major theme during the forty days between His resurrection and ascension.
         a. It was the one thing they must not neglect!
      2. Likewise, it must be our major theme before His soon coming (Ac 1:9; Mt 24:14).
         a. It is one thing we must not neglect.

II. EACH TIME JESUS' GAVE HIS GREAT COMMISSION HE CONNECTED IT WITH A PROMISE OF THE SPIRIT'S POWER OR PRESENCE.
   A. Let's look again at each Great Commission statement:
      1. John 20:21-22
         a. Jesus first said, "As the Father has sent me…"
         b. He then breathed on them and said, "Receive…"
      2. Matthew 28:18-20
         a. Jesus first said, "Go ye therefore and…"

    b. He then promised, "And lo, I am with you…" (This was a promise of the coming Spirit; compare Jn 14:16-18.)
   3. Mark 16:15-16
    a. Jesus first commanded, "Go into all the world…"
    b. He then promised, "And these signs will…" (This is a reference to the power of the Spirit as is later demonstrated in the book of Acts).
   4. Luke 24:46-49
    a. Jesus first stated, "Repentance and forgiveness…"
    b. He then commanded, " Stay in the city…"
   5. Acts 1:8
    a. Jesus said, "You will be my witnesses…"
    b. But He first said, "You will receive power…" (see also vv. 4-5).
 B. Note again how with every giving of the Great Commission Jesus promised His power or presence to go with those who would obey.
   1. That promise remains in effect today.

III. HOW SHOULD WE RESPOND TO THESE POWERFUL TRUTHS?
 A. We must recommit ourselves to obeying Christ's command to take the gospel to all nations.
 B. We must be filled and refilled with the Spirit so that we may be empowered to effectively obey Christ's command.

Conclusion and Altar Call
 1. Come now
 2. Commit yourself to helping to fulfill Christ's commission.
 3. Be filled with the Spirit.

[DRM]

48. Greater Works than These

Sermon in a Sentence: All believers should participate in the mission of Christ by the power of the Holy Spirit.

Sermon Purpose: That believers be filled with the Spirit and become active participants in reaching the nations for Christ.

Text: John 14:12

Introduction
1. Jesus made this statement at the climax of His mission on earth, just hours before His betrayal and crucifixion.
2. Jesus was preparing His disciples for what was about to take place.
3. In light of these facts, let us consider the powerful and important declaration Jesus made at that time.
4. From this declaration we will learn some important truths for our lives today:

I. THE IMPORTANCE OF JESUS' DECLARATION
   A. Different versions translate the Greek word *amen* as "verily, verily" ; "truly, truly"; or "I tell you the truth."
      1. It was a solemn declaration to emphasize and strengthen the impact of his words.
   B. Everything Jesus said is important; however, He emphasized some things to cause us to pay special attention to them.

II. THE UNIVERAL NATURE OF JESUS' DECLARATION
   A. Jesus spoke these words to His twelve disciples on the night He was betrayed. "I say to you …"
   B. But this declaration was clearly intended for all Christ's followers *("Whoever* believes in me. . .")

III. THE GOAL OF JESUS' DECLARATION
   A. His goal is that every believer will participate in His work. *("Whoever believes … will also do the works that I do.")*
   B. What works did Jesus do?
      1. He preached the good news of the kingdom of God and called people to repent and be saved.
      2. He healed the sick, and cast out demon spirits.
      3. He transformed people's lives.
   C. His goal, however, is more than just participation, but that we will actually increase His work: *"greater works than these…"*

IV. THE PROMISE OF POWER TO FULFILL JESUS DECLARATION

- A. Jesus said that we would continue to do His work
  "… because I am going to the father…"
  1. But not in our on power.
- B. The key to understanding this statement is found in what Jesus explained next to the disciples.
  1. Read John 14:16-18
  2. John 16:7: *"It is to your advantage that I go away, for if I do not go away, the Helper will not come to you."*
  3. But when the Spirit came He would be poured out upon all believers everywhere and fill them with God's power.
  4. It was for our good because Jesus was physically only with His disciples in one place.
- C. Jesus fulfilled his promise
  1. On the Day of Pentecost He poured out the Holy Spirit on the church.
  2. The book of Acts shows us the pattern in the early church: *When people became followers of Christ they were also powerfully baptized in the Holy Spirit and used by God to continue the work of Christ.*
  3. Even now Jesus wants everyone of His followers to be filled with the Spirit and continue His work.

V. HOW SHOULD WE RESPOND TO THESE TRUTHS?
- A. First, we should respond in faith.
  1. Jesus said, "Whoever, *believes*..."
  2. Faith is the key to responding correctly to God.
  3. We must believe that…
     a. … the work of Christ is the most important work there is.
     b. … God will fill us with the Holy Spirit and work powerfully through us to witness and save souls.
- B. Next, We should fully commit ourselves to Christ's mission.
- C. Finally, We should pray to be filled with the Holy Spirit.
  1. Jesus promised that He would do anything we ask in His name (vv. 13-14).
  2. We should begin by asking Him to fill us with the Holy Spirit and power to do His work (Lk 11:9-13).
  3. After we have received the Holy Spirit, we must maintain His presence through continually seeking Him in prayer.

Conclusion and Altar Call

Let's come and ask God to fill us with the Spirit and continue Christ's work through us in proclaiming the gospel.

[MT]

49. The Holy Spirit and Soul Winning

Sermon in a Sentence: The power of the Holy Spirit is a requirement for effective preaching that will bring sinners to repentance and salvation.

Sermon Purpose: To motivate preachers to seek the continual fullness and power of the Holy Spirit beginning now.

Text: Acts 2:14 - 41

Introduction
1. We all know that there are many preachers in our generation.
   a. However, it is one thing to preach, but it is another thing to preach effectively.
   b. Effective preaching is the kind of preaching that brings a harvest of souls into God's kingdom.
   c. Without the power of the Holy Spirit, the effectiveness of the preacher is limited to his own ability.
   d. For effective preaching to take place the preacher must involve the Holy Spirit, who is the Lord of the Harvest.
2. On the Day of Pentecost Peter was baptized in the Holy Spirit and then stood up and under the anointing power of the Spirit he preached a powerful message resulting in 3000 conversions.
3. There are three ways the Holy Spirit enables us to win souls:

I. HE REVEALS THE SECRET OF PEOPLE'S HEARTS.
   A. They are convicted by the revelation of God's message to them and so repent and accept the Lord Jesus Christ (Ac 2:37; 1Co 14:25).
   B. Many testify of how, when they heard the gospel being preached, they felt as if the preacher was speaking directly to them and knew everything about them.
   C. The Holy Spirit knows all things, and He speaks to sinners through His Spirit-anointed preachers (1Co 2:10-13).

II. HE DEMONSTRATES THE POWER OF GOD AS A SIGN OF GOD'S PRESENCE.
   A. On the Day of Pentecost, when the 120 were filled with the Spirit, a miracle happened, they began to speak in languages they did not previously know.
      1. Hearing this the people asked, "What does this mean?"
      2. This opened the door for Peter to declare the gospel to them.
   B. Jesus promised that signs would follow those who preach the word (Mk 16:17).

    C. Jesus did great things because of the power of the Holy Spirit (Ac 10:38).
        1. When people see such signs, even if they previously doubted the word, they will be compelled to believe.
        2. If you are filled with the Holy Spirit, God will perform signs through your ministry that will demonstrate His reality and presence and convince unbelievers to repent (Ac 1:8).

III. HE GIVES SPIRITUAL UNDERSTANDING TO PEOPLE SO THAT THEY MAY BE ABLE TO RESPOND TO THE PROMISES IN THE WORD OF GOD.
    A. Read Eph 1:17-18.
    B. Natural man is blind to the truth, but the Holy Spirit opens the eyes of the blind and reveals God's truth so we can understand it (1Co 2:12-16).

Conclusion and Altar Call
Let us come and seek a fresh infilling of the Holy Spirit so that his power will work in our preaching and enable us to reach the lost with the gospel of Jesus Christ.

[EC]

50. The Holy Spirit and the Ministry of the Church

Sermon in a Sentence: The Holy Spirit must be understood and accepted for the church to accomplish the work of the ministry.
Sermon Purpose: To encourage people to give the Holy Spirit His rightful place in the church.
Text: John 16:7-15; Acts 5:3-4; 13:2

Introduction
1. The Holy Spirit is the "Executive of the Godhead" working out God's purpose in and through the church today.
   a. Relegating Him to the background can only spell doom for the church.
2. In this message we will acquaint ourselves with the person of the Holy Spirit, and then we will highlight His importance and work.

I. UNDERSTANDING THE HOLY SPIRIT
A. The Holy Spirit is a Person (that is, He possess intelligence, emotion, and volition.
   1. The Bible presents the Holy Spirit as...
      1. ... having a mind and will (Ro 8:27, 1Co 12:11).
      2. ... teaching (Jn 14:26).
      3. ... witnessing (Col 4:6; Ro 8:15-16).
      4. ... interceding (Ro 8:26).
      5. ... speaking and commanding (Rev 2:7, Ac 16:6-7).
      6. ... testifying (Jn 15:26).
   2. He may be grieved (Eph 4:30).
   3. He may be lied to (Eph 4:30).
B. The Holy Spirit is God.
   1. He has divine attributes:
      a. He is eternal (Heb 9:14).
      b. He is omnipresent (Ps 139:7 – 10).
      c. He is omnipotent (Lk 1:35).
      d. He is omniscient (1Co 2:10, 11).
   2. He does divine works:
      a. Creation (Ge 11:2; Job 33:4).
      b. Resurrection (Ro 8:11).
   3. Has coordinate rank with the Father and the Son (1Co 12; 4-6; 2Co 13:14; Mt 28:19; Rev 1:4).

II. THE IMPORTANCE AND FUNCTIONS OF THE HOLY SPIRIT IN THE WORK OF THE CHURCH
A. He is the agent of salvation.
   1. He convicts of sin (Jn 16:7-8).

  2. He reveals the truth about Christ (Jn 14:16, 26).
  3. He gives the new birth (Jn 3:3-6).
  4. He brings believers into the body of Christ (1Co12:13).
 B. He is the agent of sanctification.
  1. Believers are indwelt by the Spirit whereupon they come under His sanctifying influence (Ro 8: 9; 1Cor 6:19).
  2. He sanctifies, cleanses, leads and motivates believers to live holy lives.
  3. He delivers from sin (Ro 8:2-4; Gal 5:16-17; 2Th 2:13).
  4. He tells believers they are God's children (Ro 8:16).
  5. He helps believers in worship (Ac 10:46).
  6. He helps us in prayer and intercession (Ro 8:26-27).
  7. He produces Christ-like graces of character that glorify Christ (Gal 5:22-23; 1Pe 1:2).
  8. He is the believers' divine teacher (1Co 2: 9-16), guiding them into all truth (Jn 16:13; 14:26; 1).
  9. He reveals Jesus to believers and guides them into close fellowship and oneness with Jesus (Jn 14:16-18; 16:14).
  10. He continually imparts God's love to us (Ro 5: 5).
  11. He gives joy, comfort and help (Jn 14:16; 1Th 1:6).
 C. He is the agent of service.
  1. He empowers believers for witness (Ac. 1:8).
  2. He bestows on believers spiritual gifts.
   a. To manifest the grace, power and love of the Spirit among His people (1Co 12:4-7; 12:25; Ro 15:15 18, 19; Eph 4:8).
   b. To make the preaching of the gospel effective by supernaturally confirming the message (Mk.16:15-20; Ac 14:8-18; 16:16-18; 19:4-20).
   c. To meet human needs and to strengthen and build the church and individual believers (1Co 12:7,14-30; 14:3,12,26; 1Ti 1:5).
   d. To wage effective spiritual war against Satan and the forces of evil (Isa 61:1; Ac 3:5-7; 26:18; Eph 6: 11-12).
  3. He directs the mission of the church (Ac 13:2,4).
  4. He appoints workers for the harvest (Ac 20:28).

Conclusion and Altar Call
 In light of all these facts the church must give the Holy Spirit His rightful place. Let us acknowledge Him as such and allow Him His full functions.

[CO]

51. Jesus' Blueprint for Building a Pentecostal Church

Sermon in a Sentence: We must follow Christ's plan for building His church.

Sermon Purpose: To help believers understand Christ's plan to build His church, and then lead them to be filled with the Spirit in order that they might follow His plan.

Text: Luke 24:45-49

Introduction
1. A blueprint is a plan to build something.
2. In our text Jesus gives us His blueprint for building a Pentecostal church.
3. If we will follow His plan, He will build His church through us.
4. This plan includes three basic elements:

I. **THE MESSAGE THE CHURCH MUST PROCLAIM** (vv. 46-47a)
   A. We must proclaim the gospel, which includes the following:
      1. Christ suffered and died for our sins (v. 46a)
      2. Christ rose from the dead on the third day (v. 46b).
      3. Those who repent of their sins and put their faith in Christ will be forgiven (vv. 47a, Ro 10:9).
   B. This message must always be at the center of our preaching, because it is…
      1. … the power of God for salvation (Ro 1:16; 1Co 1:18).
      2. … the only hope for sinners (Jn 14:6, Ac 4:12).

II. **THE MISSION THE CHURCH MUST FULFILL** (v. 47b-48).
   A. We must preach this message in Christ's name (v. 47).
      1. We do not preach in our own name or authority but in the authority of Jesus' name (Mt 28:18-20).
   B. We must preach this message to all nations (v. 47).
      1. We must begin in our "Jerusalem" and proceed to the ends of the earth (Ac 1:8).
   C. God's primary mission for each of us is to be His witness (v. 48).
   D. Will you accept your part in the mission of God?
      1. Will you preach the message of the gospel to the lost?
      2. Will you participate in taking this message to all nations?

III. **THE MIGHT THE CHURCH CAN EXPECT TO RECEIVE** (v.49).
   A. The source of this might is the Holy Spirit.
      1. He comes into believers and fills them with His power.
      2. The Father promised to send the Holy Spirit (Joel 2:28).

      3. Jesus sent the Spirit on the Day of Pentecost.
      4. This promise of the gift of the Holy Spirit is for every believer (Ac 2:17, 38-39).
      5. We each need to be filled with the Holy Spirit in the same way as believers were filled in the book of Acts.
  B. We all need the might of the Spirit.
      1. Jesus told the disciples not to leave Jerusalem until they were clothed with the power from on high (Lk 24:49).
      2. A person should not go out in public unclothed! In the same way, a Christian should not go out into the world without being clothed with the power of the Holy Spirit.
      3. Without the power of the Spirit we will not be able to adequately preach the message and fulfill the mission Christ has given us.
  C. The Spirit's might is neither financial, intellectual nor social power; it is rather spiritual power.
      a. The Spirit changes our way of thinking and acting.
      b. He enables us to proclaim the message of the cross effectively and with courage.
      c. He gives us discernment, wisdom, and other important gifts.
      d. He helps us live holy lives so our words and actions will, together, witness for Christ.

Conclusion and Altar Call
1. Come and commit your life to God's mission of preaching Christ to the whole world.
2. Then be filled with the Holy Spirit so you will have the power to do so

[DG]

52. Jesus' "Not-So-Famous" Last Words

Sermon in a Sentence: We should understand and obey the "not-so-famous" last words of Jesus.

Sermon Purpose: That Christians understand the importance of being baptized in the Holy Spirit and that they receive the experience today.

Text: Acts 1:1-11

Introduction
1. This passage records the very last words of Jesus before He returned to heaven (vv. 4-8).
2. I say they are "not-so-famous" because many Christians either do not know about or do not choose to obey them.
3. Today we will learn these words and, hopefully, obey them.
4. We should understand six important truths about these last words of Jesus: (They were …)

I. **SPIRIT-INSPIRED WORDS** (v. 2: "after giving instructions through the Holy Spirit")
   A. Jesus performed His entire ministry under the direction of the Holy Spirit (Lk 4:17-18; Ac 10:38).
   B. Here, after His resurrection, He is still speaking by the Spirit.
   C. We, too, have been called to minister in the Spirit (Ac 1:8).

II. **KINGDOM WORDS** (v. 3: "spoke about the kingdom of God")
   A. Jesus came announcing the kingdom of God (Mk 1:15).
   B. The kingdom of God comes in power (Mk 9:1; 1Co 4:20).
   C. Our job is to advance God's kingdom on the earth (Mt 24:14).

III. **AUTHORITATIVE WORDS** (v. 4: "he gave them this command")
   A. Jesus has commanded us to be filled with the Holy Spirit (v. 4; see also Eph 5:18).
   B. The experience of the baptism in the Holy Spirit is too important to be left as an option.
   C. We must all obey His command today (Jn 14:15; Mt 28:20).

IV. **EMPOWERING WORDS** (v. 8: "you will receive power when the Holy Spirit comes on you")
   A. Christ has commissioned every Christian to be His witness (Lk 24:44-46).
   B. The primary purpose of the baptism in the Holy Spirit is empowerment to witness (Ac 1:8, 4:31).
   C. This empowering comes "when the Holy Spirit comes on us."

V. **COMMISSIONING WORDS** (v. 8: "you will be my witnesses ... to the ends of the earth")
   A. Christ wants to empower us with His Spirit so that we can fulfill the Great Commission (Lk 24:47-49).
   B. The Great Commission is Christ's command to take the gospel to all nations (Mt 28:19-20; Mk 16:1-16).
   C. We must each be filled with the Spirit to participate in Christ's mission (Ac 1:4-5).

VI. **DEPARTING WORDS** (v. 9: "After he said this, he was taken up before their very eyes, and a cloud hid him from their sight")
   A. These were Jesus last words.
   B. They are, therefore, very important words.
   C. We must obey His words today and be filled with the Holy Spirit and preach the gospel to the lost.

Conclusion and Altar Call
   1. Come now to be filled with the Holy Spirit.
   2. How can one be filled with the Spirit?
      a. Ask in faith (Lk 11:9, 13).
      b. Receive by faith (Lk 11:10; Mk 11:24).
      c. Speak in faith (Ac 2:4; Jn 7:37-38).

[DRM]

53. Lessons Learned from Acts 2

Sermon in a Sentence: Let the Holy Spirit fill you and change your life today in the same way that He filled and changed the lives of the disciples in the book of Acts.

Sermon Purpose: That believers will be filled and/or refilled with the Holy Spirit and empowered as Christ's witnesses.

Text: Acts 2:1-46

Introduction
1. We have just read about the Day of Pentecost.
2. Pentecost set a pattern for the rest of the Age of the Spirit.
3. What are some lessons we can learn from what took place on the Day of Pentecost?

I. **LIKE THE DISCIPLES BEFORE PENTECOST, WE MUST LONG FOR THE POWER OF THE HOLY SPIRIT IN OUR CHURCH AND IN OUR INDIVIDUAL LIVES.**
   A. We must long for Him to manifest Himself in our midst (vv.1-3).
   B. We must long for Him to fill us with His power and presence today (v.4).
   C. If we will do these things, we can expect our city to take note just as Jerusalem took note (vv. 5-13).

II. **LIKE THE DISCIPLES AT PENTECOST, WE MUST UNDERSTAND WHAT THE SPIRIT'S COMING MEANS IN OUR LIVES AND IN OUR CHURCH.**
   A. It means that we are following in the biblical pattern set down by God for all believers (vv.14-18).
   B. It means that we can expect a new revelation of Jesus in our lives and ministries (vv.22-24; 32-33, 36).
   C. It means that we will become a part of God's great last-days prophetic community (vv.17-18, 4 with 14).

III. **LIKE THE DISCIPLES AT PENTECOST, WE CAN EXPECT OUR CHURCH AND OUR LIVES TO BE TRANSFORMED BY THE SPIRIT'S COMING IN POWER.**
   A. Sinners will sense the presence of the Spirit in our midst, and they will be convinced and convicted of their sins (v. 37).
   B. Our altars will be filled with people calling on the name of Christ (v. 41).
   C. Our church will become strong and powerful.
      1. Strong in unity (v. 42).
      2. Strong in spiritual power (v. 43).

3. Strong in love (vv. 44-45).
4. Filled with joy (v. 46).

Conclusion and Altar Call
1. We must be like the believers on the Day of Pentecost.
2. Come and be baptized in the Holy Spirit now!

[DRM]

54. Men Preaching Everywhere
The Role of Spirit-anointed Laymen in Advancing the Kingdom of God

Sermon in a Sentence: God wants to fill laymen with the Spirit and use them to preach the gospel everywhere.
Sermon Purpose: That Christian laymen might be filled with the Spirit and share the gospel with the lost.
Text: Acts 8:1-5

Introduction
1. What should be the role of Spirit-filled laymen in the church today?
2. Traditionally, it has been very limited, but what does the Bible teach?
3. From the story of the Samaritan revival we learn three lessons:

I. **GOD HAS PLACED A "CALL TO PREACH" THE WORD ON THE LIFE OF EVERY CHRISTIAN LAYMAN.**
   A. Those who "went everywhere preaching the word" in our text were not the apostles but Spirit-filled laymen (v. 4).
   B. The book of Acts tells of Spirit-anointed laymen who powerfully preached the gospel to the lost.
      1. *Stephen* was the instrument God used to prepare Paul's heart to receive the gospel (Ac 6-7).
      2. *Philip* lead the great revival in Samaria (Ac 8:4-17).
   C. We must come to a truly Pentecostal understanding of the call to preach the gospel.
      1. There is truly a special call into full-time ministry.
      2. Nevertheless, it is also true that all Christians are called to witness for Christ.
      3. In this sense everyone who has been baptized in the Holy Spirit is "called to preach" the gospel (Ac 1:8).

II. **GOD IS AT WORK DIRECTING OUR LIVES TO WHERE HE WANTS US TO PREACH THE GOSPEL.**
   A. In our text they went *everywhere* preaching the gospel.
      1. For them "everywhere" was "throughout the regions of Judea and Samaria" (Ac 8:1).
      2. For you "everywhere" could be to the boys in your own church, the place where you live and work, the next village, your home village, an unreached community in your city, the college campus near you, or any other place people need to hear about Christ.

3. For Jesus "everywhere" included "the remotest parts of the earth" (Ac 1:8; Mk 16:15-16).
  B. The Spirit will direct you to where He wants you to preach the gospel.
    1. He directed the Jerusalem disciples through allowing persecution to come (v. 1).
    2. He can direct you in many other ways:
      a. He may speak to you directly.
      b. He may put you near an existing need.
      c. He may make you aware of a need through circumstances (Mt 9:36-37).
      d. Sometimes our jobs will take us to where Christ needs to be preached.

III. **IN ORDER TO FULFILL GOD'S CALL ON OUR LIVES WE MUST EACH BE FILLED WITH THE HOLY SPIRIT.**
  A. The infilling of the Spirit gave the laymen in our text the power they needed to do what they did.
    1. Even though they were refugees "they went everywhere preaching the word" (v. 4).
    2. They did this because they were committed to Christ and His mission and they had been filled with the Holy Spirit (Ac 2:4; 4:31).
    3. The same was true for Stephen and Philip (Ac 6:3-10).
  B. We, too, must each be powerfully baptized with the Holy Spirit and empowered as Christ's witnesses (Ac 1:8).
  C. How can we each be filled with the Spirit today?
    1. By asking Christ to fill us (Lk 11:9-13).
    2. By believing Christ's promise (Mk 11:24).

Conclusion and Altar Call
  1. Come and be filled with the Spirit today.
  2. Then go out and preach the gospel to the lost wherever you find them.

[DRM]

55. The Missionary Purpose of Pentecost

Sermon in a Sentence: The biblical account of Pentecost reveals that the purpose of the baptism in the Holy Spirit is empowerment for missional witness.

Sermon Purpose: That believers may be filled with the Spirit and become effective witnesses for Christ.

Text: Acts 1:8; 2:1-12

Introduction
1. The purpose of the baptism in the Holy Spirit is empowerment for witness at home and around the world (Ac 1:8).
2. This truth is illustrated by the events of the Day of Pentecost.
3. Six facts demonstrate that the purpose of Pentecost is empowerment for global witness:

I. THE PROMISE OF PENTECOST.
   A. The promise of Pentecost is found in Acts 1:8.
   B. According to this promise of Jesus, the primary purpose of the baptism in the Holy Spirit is to empower Christians for witness at home and to the nations.

II. THE TIMING OF PENTECOST.
   A. The Spirit was poured out on the Day of Pentecost (Ac 2:1).
   B. In the Old Testament the Day of Pentecost was a Harvest Festival (Ex 23:16; 34:22).
   C. The timing was not coincidental: Pentecost marked the beginning of God's great worldwide harvest.

III. THE SETTING OF PENTECOST.
   A. Note Acts 2:5: "There were dwelling in Jerusalem, Jews from every nation under heaven."
   B. On the Day of Pentecost God arranged an international gathering because He wanted us to understand that the purpose of Pentecost is to empower the church to reach people of all nations.
   C. Missions began immediately upon receiving the Holy Spirit, (i.e., Peter preached and 3000 people from many nations were saved, Ac 2:41).

IV. THE SIGN OF PENTECOST.
   A. Acts 2:4 says, "They all began to speak in other tongues."

    B. God choose Gentile tongues because He wanted us to understand the purpose of the baptism in the Holy Spirit was missionary witness.

V. PETER'S EXPLANATION OF PENTECOST.
(Note how Peter emphasized three things:)
    A. Peter's first emphasis: "the last days" (Ac 2:17).
        1. The church is a "last days" community.
        2. The last days is a time of harvest!
    B. Peter's second emphasis, "all flesh" (Ac 12:17b, 39).
        1. The baptism in the Holy Spirit is for all people everywhere.
        2. God wants to empower all to be His missionary witnesses.
    C. Peter's third emphasis: Spirit-inspired proclamation (Ac 2:17-18).
        1. The church is to be a community of Spirit-anointed witnesses for Jesus Christ (Ac 2:21).

VI. THE RESULTS OF PENTECOST.
    A. The immediate result of the disciples receiving the Spirit at Pentecost was powerful Spirit-anointed witness.
        1. Peter preached and 3,000 were saved (Ac 2:41).
        2. People continued to be saved (Ac 2:47).
    B. Throughout the book of Acts, every time the Spirit was poured out it resulted in powerful witness.

Conclusion and Altar Call
1. God wants you to participate in His mission.
2. But first you must be filled with the Spirit
3. Come now and receive the Holy Spirit.

[DRM]

56. Mobilizing Spirit-Empowered Churches

Sermon in a Sentence: We must all mobilize our churches as effective Spirit-empowered church-planting churches.
Sermon Purpose: That church leaders will commit themselves to lead their churches into effective Spirit-empowered church planting.
Texts: Numbers 11:16-17; Luke 24:46-49

Introduction
1. It is God's will that every church be effective in evangelism and church planting.
2. In this message we will seek to answer the question, "How can pastors and church leaders mobilize their churches for Spirit-empowered evangelism and church planting?"
3. We will look at the examples of two great leaders who mobilized their followers for Spirit-empowered ministry.
   a. First, Moses, the great leader of Israel.
   b. Second, Jesus, our great leader of the church.
4. Each one will serve as a great example for us.
   a. We will see how each mobilized his followers.
   b. We will apply what we learn to our own situations.

I. MOSES MOBILIZED THE ELDERS OF ISRAEL (Nu 11:1-30).
   A. Moses had a problem.
      1. The people were complaining (vv. 1-9).
      2. In desperation Moses cried out to God (vv. 10-15).
   B. God gave Moses a four-part solution for his problem.
      1. First, Moses was to ensure that he himself was full of the Spirit (implied in v. 25).
      2. Next, He was to carefully choose men to help him (v. 16)
      3. Third, God would fill each of them with His Spirit and empower them to help Moses in the work (v. 17).
      4. Finally, all along they would need to trust God to supernaturally provide for their needs (vv. 17-23).
   C. Moses obeyed God, and the work was accomplished.
      1. God came down and took His Spirit who was on Moses and put Him on the seventy elders (v. 25).
      2. They prophesied and were empowered to help Moses.
   D. From this story we learn some important lessons:
      1. Like Moses, we must ourselves be filled with the Spirit.
      2. Like Moses, we must seek God for His guidance.
      3. Like Moses, we must carefully choose faithful people to help in the work.

4. Like Moses, we must ensure that each one is empowered by the Holy Spirit.
5. Like Moses, we must teach them about God's mission.
6. Like Moses, we must mobilize them and use them to accomplish the work.

II. JESUS MOBILIZED HIS CHURCH IN MUCH THE SAME WAY.
A. Jesus carefully chose those who would help Him.
 1. He knew that He would need others to help Him accomplish His work of reaching all nations with the gospel (Lk 24:46-48).
 2. He spent the night in prayer before choosing those who would help Him (Lk 6:12-13).
B. Jesus then mobilized them to fulfill the mission of God.
 1. He was Himself filled with the Spirit (Lk 4:17-18).
 2. He spent much time with them, teaching them about His ways, His mission, and His work.
 3. He ensured that they were each empowered by the Holy Spirit (Lk 24:49, see also Ac 1:4-8).
 4. He commissioned them and sent them into the work (Lk 24:48; Mk 16:15-16).

C. TODAY, THAT SAME GOSPEL HAS COME ALL THE WAY TO US.
A. Like Jesus we must mobilize the church to take the gospel to others.
B. We must ensure that our churches are filled with the Spirit and mobilized to plant churches in areas where Christ is not known.

Conclusion and Altar Call
1. Come now and be filled and refilled with the Spirit.
2. Come and commit yourself to planting other Spirit-empowered churches.

[LC]

57. Not By Might, Nor Power, But By My Spirit

Sermon in a Sentence: God's mission to save the lost and build His church will only be accomplished by the power of the Spirit working through His people.

Sermon Purpose: To see people filled with the Spirit and empowered for God's mission.

Text: Zechariah 4:1-14

Introduction
1. God's mission is to save people from every nation and build His kingdom through them (Ac 1:8).
2. Under Zerubbabel's leadership the Jews had returned from Babylonian exile and had begun to build a new temple. However, they had become discouraged and abandoned the work. Now, 18 years later the work remained undone.
3. In our text God revealed to Zerubbabel his need to trust the Spirit of God in order to be able to accomplish the work of rebuilding the temple (Zech. 4:6).
4. Here we learn four important truths about how God's power will work through us to accomplish His work:

I. THE BUILDING OF GOD'S TEMPLE CAN ONLY BE ACCOMPLISHED BY THE POWER OF THE SPIRIT (v. 1-6).
   A. The lampstand in this passage symbolizes the nation of Israel which God had appointed as a light to the nations.
      1. God called Abraham and his descendants to bless them, and through them, bless the nations (Ge 12:1-3).
      2. Israel disobeyed God, and their light did not shine.
      3. Now God was reestablishing the light through the remnant.
      4. But they did not have the strength to accomplish the task, and for 18 years the temple remained unfinished.
   B. A word from the Lord came to Zerubbabel (v. 6).
      1. It was not just a suggestion.
      2. It was God's message of how He works
      3. That is, "Not by might, nor power, but by my Spirit."
   C. God's temple can only be built by the power of the Spirit.
      1. Zerubbabel was rebuilding the temple in Jerusalem.
      2. We are now the temple of the Holy Spirit (Eph 2:19-22).
   D. God's word to Zerubbabel is still true for us today:
      1. Jesus said "I will build my church" (Mt 16:18).
      2. This will only be accomplished when God's people rely on and seek the Spirit's power.

3. This is why Jesus promised the Holy Spirit to all believers (Lk 24:49; Ac 1:4-5, 8).

II. **WHEN YOU ARE FILLED WITH THE HOLY SPIRIT, NO OBSTACLE IS TOO GREAT** (vv. 7-9).
   A. There will always be obstacles when we commit our lives to God's mission of winning the lost and building His church.
   B. Like Zerubbabel and the people of Israel, it is easy to become discouraged, and abandon the work.
   C. God allows us to face obstacles...
      1. … to teach us to seek the power of the Spirit (v. 6).
      2. … to help us realize that what to us are obstacles are often God's opportunities.
   D. When we are filled with the Holy Spirit there are no obstacles too great.

III. **WHEN YOU ARE FILLED WITH THE HOLY SPIRIT, NO BEGINNING IS TOO SMALL** (v. 10; Haggai 2:2-5, 9).
   A. "Who despises the day of small things?" (v. 10).
   B. "The glory of this house will be greater than the former house" (Hag 2:9).
   C. God uses small beginnings to accomplish His mission.

IV. **WHEN YOU ARE FILLED WITH THE HOLY SPIRIT, GOD CAN USE YOU NO MATTER WHO YOU ARE** (vv. 11-14).
   A. For 18 years Joshua and Zerubbabel had failed to accomplish their mission.
      1. But God did not give up on them.
      2. His word to them was to depend on the Holy Spirit.
   B. God often uses people who are weak and don't feel they are capable.
      1. When you have been filled with the Spirit God will use you no matter what has happened in the past.

Conclusion and Altar Call
1. God's plan is to save the lost and build His church.
2. He is looking for people who believe that it is "not by might, nor power, but by His Spirit."
3. Today you can filled with God's power to accomplish God's mission.
4. Come, ask and believe, and God will fill you with His Spirit.

[MT]

58 | Pentecost and World Evangelism

Sermon in a Sentence: If we are going to reach the world for Christ, we must each be empowered by the Spirit.
Sermon Purpose: That believers might be filled with the Spirit and commit themselves to participating in reaching the lost at home and around the world.
Text: Acts 1:8; 2:1-4

Introduction
1. At Pentecost God sent His Spirit to empower the church to bring His plan of redemption to the world (Ac 1:8; 2:1-4).
2. As this age draws to a close another wave of Pentecostal power has been sent.
3. Its purpose is to empower the church to complete the Great Commission before Jesus comes again (Mt. 24:14).
4. Today, as at the beginning, we must each be baptized in the Holy Spirit to effectively participate in God's mission.
5. Let's look at three important concepts that flow from this fact:

I. THE IMPORTANCE OF PENTECOSTAL EXPERIENCE
   A. There is reality in the baptism in the Holy Spirit.
      1. It is more than a mere doctrine.
      2. It is divine power resulting in an inward impulse to fulfill the divine purpose.
   B. In Latin America it is estimated that two-thirds of all evangelical Christians have Pentecostal backgrounds.
      1. It is the power of the Holy Spirit that makes these churches multiply and grow.
      2. When baptized in the Spirit, new believers quickly become proclaimers of the gospel.

II. THE IMPORTANCE OF PENTECOSTAL MINISTRY
   A. Through the power of the Holy Spirit we can confront and defeat the enemy.
      1. Christ's witnesses must often confront Satan's power.
      2. Pentecostal missionaries and church planters step out in faith to challenge these evil powers.
      3. ILLUS: Like Elijah at Mount Carmel (1Ki 18:24).
      4. When God triumphs through the power of the Holy Spirit, people's hearts are opened to receive the gospel.
   B. Pentecostal outpourings produce indigenous churches.
      1. Around the world the great indigenous church movements are, for the most part, Pentecostal.

2. Having experienced the baptism in the Holy Spirit, believers find the spiritual direction and necessary power to move forward.

III. THE NECESSITY OF MAINTAINING OUR PENTECOSTAL FOCUS
A. We as Pentecostals must maintain our goals and forge ahead along the lines that have brought victory and blessing in the past.
   1. We must resist the temptation to leave the life of faith and depend upon human effort.
   2. We must maintain our trust in the Holy Spirit and His ability to empower us to do the work.
B. We Pentecostals face certain dangers, such as,
   1. The danger of *doctrinal deviation.*
      a. Winds of new doctrine often blow through the Pentecostal church.
      b. However, we must hold to Scripture as our source of truth and practice.
   2. The danger of the *"perfecting syndrome."*
      a. Spirit baptism does bring sanctification and blessing.
      b. We must not, however, forget that its primary purpose is to focus us on the needs of lost humanity.
   3. The danger of *leaving behind the dynamics of the Spirit* in favor of human structures.
      a. Structure can be helpful.
      b. However, we must be careful not to give structure so much emphasis that we lose the dynamics of the Holy Spirit.

Conclusion and Altar Call
Come now to be filled with the Spirit and empowered to participate in Christ's mission to reach the lost around the world.

[MH]

* Editor's Note: This sermon outline is adapted from an article by the same name by Melvin L. Hodges appearing in *Paraklete,* Spring 1981.

59. The Power of Pentecost

Sermon in a Sentence: The power of Pentecost will change you into one of Christ's fiery evangelists.
Sermon Purpose: That believers will be filled with the Spirit and become Christ's "fiery evangelist."
Text: Acts 2:1-4

Introduction
1. The power of Pentecost transformed the disciples from little-known peasants into Spirit-anointed prophets, from simple fishermen into fiery evangelists.
2. The power of Pentecost can change you from what you are today into Christ's powerful witness.
3. We must each experience the power of Pentecost today.
4. Notice these three powerful truths about the power of Pentecost:

I. THE POWER OF PENTECOST WAS PUBLIC.
A. The Spirit was poured out publically.
 1. That is, He was poured out on all of the 120 disciples.
 2. Notice that "they were *all* filled" (v. 4).
B. The events of Pentecost brought a multitude to hear and believe the gospel.
 1. A great crowd gathered.
 2. Peter preached the gospel and 3000 were saved.
C. The purpose of Pentecost is for many to hear and believe the gospel at home and throughout the world (Ac 1:8).

II. THE POWER OF PENTECOST WAS PERSONAL.
A. Each of the 120 disciples had a personal Pentecostal experience with the Spirit.
 1. If all were filled, then *each* was filled.
 2. Notice how an individual tongue of fire sat upon "each one" of them (v. 5).
B. At Pentecost the pattern was established.
 1. The baptism in the Holy Spirit is a normative experience for all believers.
 2. It is an empowerment for witness (Ac 1:8).
 3. The baptism in the Holy Spirit is for you today.

III. THE POWER OF PENTECOST WAS A PRESENCE.
A. Jesus had promised His disciples His continuing presence:
 1. In giving to them the Great Commission, He promised, "Surely I am with you always, to the very end of the age" (Mt 28:18-20; note v. 20).

2. In the upper room before His crucifixion, He promised, "I will not leave you as orphans; I will come to you" (Jn 14:16-18; note v. 18).
3. Both of these promises were first fulfilled at Pentecost.
4. The Holy Spirit makes Christ ever-present.
B. Whenever the church allows the Spirit to move, a dynamic witness takes place.
1. Jesus promised power to witness (Ac 1:8).
2. The 120 were clothed with power from on high and transformed into flaming evangelists (Lk 24:49).
C. The dynamic witness of the church that began at Pentecost continues today.
1. Allow it to continue in you.

Conclusion and Altar Call
1. God wants to give you the power of Pentecost, the power to be His witness.
2. Come and be filled with the Holy Spirit today.
   a. Let's invite the Holy Spirit to come upon *all* of us.
   b. Let's invite the Holy Spirit to come upon *each* of us.
   c. Invite the Holy Spirit to come upon you personally.

[GRC]

* Adapted from: Raymond G. Carlson, *The Acts Story: The Work of the Holy Spirit in the Early Church*. Springfield, MO: Gospel Publishing House, 1978. page 13.

60. Power with Purpose

Sermon in a Sentence: God wants to give you the Spirit to empower you to be His witness.

Sermon Purpose: That believers may understand the purpose of the baptism in the Holy Spirit and then be baptized in the Holy Spirit and empowered as Christ's witnesses.

Text: Acts 1:1-8

Introduction
1. In these last words of Jesus He left His church with a purpose and power.
    a. *Its purpose:* "you will be my witnesses … to the ends of the earth" (Ac 1:8b; ref. Mk 15:15-16).
    b. *Its power:* "But you will receive power when the Holy Spirit comes upon you" (v. 8a; ref. Lk 24:48-49).
2. This text answers three questions about this "power with purpose":

I. WHO IS THE POWER FOR?
A. The power is for "You." (Note: *"You* will receive power")
B. This statement can apply to three "You's":
   1. *The specific you:* The first disciples (Ac 1:8).
   2. *The universal you:* All believers for the entire church age (Ac 2:38-39).
   3. *The personal you:* You who are here today!
C. The power is not so much given *to* you as *through* you, to take the gospel to the nations!

II. WHEN IS THE POWER RECEIVED?
(It is received "when the Holy Spirit comes upon you")
A. The power was first received by the disciples when the Holy Spirit came upon them at Pentecost (Ac 2:1-4).
B. The power is received subsequent to salvation.
   1. The disciples were already saved when they received it.
   2. Spirit baptism is an experience separate from salvation.
   3. Its purpose is empowerment for mission.
C. Throughout Acts the Spirit continued to come upon other believers with the same results—powerful witness.
   1. A second Jerusalem Outpouring (Ac 4:31-33).
   2. Saul of Tarsus (Ac 9:17-20).
   3. Believers in Ephesus (Ac 19:6-7; 10).
D. The Spirit will come upon you today.

III. WHY IS THE POWER GIVEN?
(Note the phrase "and you will be my witnesses")
- A. The power is given to empower disciples for witness!
    1. At Pentecost it resulted in powerful Spirit-anointed witness.
    2. 3000 were saved (Ac 2:39-41).
- B. Spirit-empowered witness is the guiding theme of Acts.
    1. See: Ac 1:21; 2:32; 5:32; 10:38-41.
- C. We have all been called to be Christ's witnesses, therefore, we must all receive the Spirit's power.

Conclusion and Altar Call
1. You can receive power with purpose today by being baptized in the Holy Spirit today.
2. How can you receive this power?
    - a. Ask in faith (Lk 11:9, 10, 13).
    - b. Receive by faith (Lk 11:10; Mk 11:24).
    - c. Speak in faith (Ac 2:4).

[DRM]

61. The Spirit's Desire for the Nations

Sermon in a Sentence: The Holy Spirit wants to empower every believer to participate in reaching the nations with the gospel.
Sermon Purpose: That believers be filled with the Spirit and become active participants in reaching the nations for Christ.
Text: Acts 1:8

Introduction
1. The Holy Spirit is the Spirit of Missions.
2. Our text reveals four truths about the Spirit's desire for the nations:

I. **THE HOLY SPIRIT DESIRES THE NATIONS.**
   A. Christ's promise in Acts 1:8 indicates that the Spirit wants all nations to hear the gospel.
      1. The rationale: If the Holy Spirit gives power to reach the nations, then He must want the nations be reached.
   B. With the coming of the Spirit comes a compulsion to proclaim Christ to the lost.
      1. The Spirit transfers Christ's power to His disciples.
      2. He also transfers to them His passion for the lost and home and to the ends of the earth.

II. **THE HOLY SPIRIT USES CHRIST'S DISCIPLES TO REACH THE ENDS OF THE EARTH.**
   A. He used the first disciples to reach their world.
      1. The book of Acts tells their story.
      2. They "turned the world upside down" (Ac 17:6, KJV).
   B. Today the Spirit chooses to use us to reach the ends of the earth.
      1. He chooses us (Jn 15:6).
      2. He fills and empowers us (Ac 1:8).
      4. He gives us a love for people (Ro 5:5).
      3. He sends us (Jn 20:21-22).

III. **THE HOLY SPIRIT GIVES POWER TO CHRIST'S DISCIPLES FOR WORLDWIDE EVANGELISM.**
   A. The power of the Spirit is essential if we are going to reach the nations (Lk 24:46-49; Ac 1:4-5).
   B. The Holy Spirit is the Great Overseer of the harvest.

IV. **THE HOLY SPIRIT EMPOWERS US FOR THE SAME PURPOSE TODAY.**
   A. We must receive the power of the Spirit today (Ac 2:39).

    B.   The power is given today for the same purpose that it was given in the beginning.
          1.   That is, for power to witness for Christ at home and around the world (Ac 1:8).
    C.   The Spirit will come upon us today just as He did on the disciples at the beginning.

Conclusion and Altar Call
1. Are you ready to receive?
2. Come now to receive the Spirit and be equipped to participate in reaching the nations with the gospel.

[JE]

62. We Must Never Forget

Sermon in a Sentence: We must never forget that, as Pentecostals, we are God's last-days, Spirit-empowered, missionary people.
Sermon Purpose: That believers will be filled with the Spirit and commit themselves to fulfilling the mission of God.
Text: Acts 1:8

Introduction
1. Our text has been called the "defining verse of true Pentecostalism."
2. More than any other text, it reminds us of who we are and why we exist.
3. As Pentecostals we must never forget the following:

I. **WE MUST NEVER FORGET WHO WE ARE: WE ARE PENTECOSTALS.**
   A. We love and appreciate very much our evangelical brothers and sisters who are faithfully preaching Christ.
   B. However, we as Pentecostals are evangelicals of a different sort.
      1. We believe that the power of God is for the church today.
      2. We believe that God wants to give every believer His power.
   C. As a result, God is blessing the Pentecostal Movement today
   D. There is, nevertheless, a misunderstanding among Pentecostals of what it really means to be a Pentecostal, therefore ...

II. **WE MUST UNDERSTAND WHAT IT MEANS TO BE TRULY PENTECOSTAL.**
   A. Pentecostalism is more than a "bless me" movement.
   B. Truly defined, Pentecostalism is a "popular, last-days, Spirit-empowered, missionary movement."
   C. Let's "unwrap" and look at each part of our definition:
      1. "True Pentecostalism is a *movement*."
         a. It is not a denomination.
         b. It is a movement (i.e., like a social movement or uprising).
      2. "True Pentecostalism is a *missionary* movement."
         a. In our text, Jesus defined true Pentecostalism as a missionary movement (Ac 1:8).
         b. Only those involved in God's mission are true Pentecostals.

3. "True Pentecostalism is a *Spirit-empowered* missionary movement."
   a. To be truly Pentecostal means to be empowered by the Spirit.
   b. This empowering comes when we are baptized in the Holy Spirit (Ac 1:8; 2:4).
   c. Jesus will give you the Holy Spirit if you will ask Him for it (Lk 9-10, 13).
4. "True Pentecostalism is a *last-days*, Spirit-empowered, missionary movement."
   a. God has poured out His Spirit in the last days (Ac 2:17-18).
   b. In scripture the "last days" is synonymous with the Age of the Spirit.
   c. Because Jesus is coming soon we must be about the Master's business (ILLUS: Ac 1:9-11).
5. "True Pentecostalism is a *popular*, last-days, Spirit-empowered, missionary movement.
   a. "Popular," that is, it is, a movement of the common people.
   b. True Pentecostalism is the "Great Democratizer."
   c. Today, all of God's people can be Spirit-anointed prophets, that is, Spirit-anointed proclaimers of the gospel (Nu 11:29; Ac 2:17-18; Ac 1:8).

III. AS AUTHENTIC PENTECOSTALS, WE MUST PUT OUR BELIEFS INTO PRACTICE.

A. We must live and minister as if we were living in the very last days of history.
B. We must get fully involved in fulfilling the Great Commission of Jesus.
C. We must all seek for and experience the empowering experience of the baptism in the Holy Spirit.
D. We must let all of God's people minister.

Conclusion and Altar Call
Come now, be filled with the Spirit and commit yourself to God's last-days mission.

[DRM]

63. What I Have I Give to You

Sermon in a Sentence: God has given us His blessing and His Spirit so we can bless others.

Sermon Purpose: That people may be filled with the Spirit and understand that God gives them His Spirit and gifts so that they may be a blessing to others.

Text: Acts 3:1-10

Introduction
1. Our text tells the story of the healing of the lame man at the Beautiful Gate.
2. Notice Peter's words, "Silver and gold have I none; *but such as I have give I thee*: In the name of Jesus Christ of Nazareth rise up and walk" (Ac 3:6, KJV).
3. What did Peter have to give away? How can we have the same, and do the same thing with it?

I. WHAT DID PETER HAVE?
A. Peter had the power of the Spirit.
   1. When he said "such as I have," he was making reference to what he received on the Day of Pentecost.
   2. At Pentecost Peter received the power of the Holy Spirit (Ac 1:8; 2:4).
   3. His Pentecostal experience resulted in a dramatic release of spiritual power, resulting in a great harvest of souls (Ac 2:41).
B. Peter had the authority of Jesus' name.
   1. Listen to Peter's words: "In the name of Jesus Christ of Nazareth, rise up and walk" (Ac 3:6).
   2. We can only use Jesus' name if we are submitted to His will and actively engaged in fulfilling His mission.
C. Peter had faith in God.
   1. At the Beautiful Gate, Peter acted in bold faith (Ac 3:6).
   2. Had he not acted in faith, and spoken in faith, the work would not have been done.
   3. As a result of being filled with the Spirit, submitting himself to the will of Christ, and acting in faith, a wonderful miracle occurred.
   4. If we will do as Peter did, we can expect the same results in our ministries today.

II. WHAT DID PETER DO WITH WHAT HE HAD?
A. He gave it away!

1. Peter understood that what he had received from God was not for him to consume for his own selfish desires.
   a. This is a problem in many churches and in the lives of many Christians today.
   b. James addressed this issue (Jas 4:2-3).
2. The primary purpose of the baptism in the Holy Spirit is so that we can give it away (Ac 1:8; 4:31, 33).

B. How did Peter go about giving away what he had?
   1. He remained full of the Spirit (see Ac 4:8).
   2. He obeyed Christ's commission to preach the gospel to the lost (Mk 16:15).
   3. He listened to and obeyed the voice of the Spirit.
   4. He acted in boldness and faith.

III. WHAT MUST WE DO ABOUT THESE ISSUES?
A. We must ensure that we have received something from God.
   1. Make sure that you have been truly born again (Jn 3:7).
   2. Make sure that you have been genuinely baptized in the Holy Spirit (Eph 5:18).
   3. Make sure that you understand how to use the power of Jesus name.
B. We must be obedient to Christ's Commission.
   1. We must be about spreading the gospel at home and abroad.
   2. As we obey, the Spirit will anoint and empower us (Jn 20:21-22).
C. We must give away what we have received.
   1. We must be ready to preach the gospel in the power of the Spirit (Ro 1:15).
   2. We must be ready to be used by the Spirit in the manifestation of spiritual gifts (1Co 12:31; 14:1).
   3. We must be ready to act in bold faith in the name of Jesus.

Conclusion and Altar Call
1. Come to be filled and refilled with the Spirit.
2. Then go out and give away what you have received.

[DRM]

64. Witnessing in the Spirit

Sermon in a Sentence: God wants you to be His Spirit-empowered witness.

Sermon Purpose: That believers be baptized in the Holy Spirit evidenced by speaking in tongues and Spirit-inspired witness.

Text: Acts 1:8; 2:1-4,14

Introduction
1. We as Pentecostals are very familiar with this passage of Scripture (Ac 2:1-4), especially with verse 4.
2. We often emphasize the fact that the 120 believers spoke in tongues as a result of their being filled with the Spirit.
   a. This is good, however, it is an incomplete understanding of what actually happened on the Day of Pentecost.
   b. Not only did the disciples speak in tongues, they also bore Spirit-empowered witness to Christ.
3. This message will address the critical, but neglected, issue of Spirit-empowered witness.

I. **A THOUGHTFUL EXAMINATION OF ACTS 2 REVEALS THAT TWO KINDS OF SPEAKING BY THE SPIRIT TOOK PLACE ON THE DAY OF PENTECOST.**
   A. First, the believers *spoke in tongues* as the Spirit enabled them.
      1. Their speaking in tongues meant that they had been filled with the Spirit, and...
         a. that they had been empowered to speak for Christ.
         b. that they had been empowered to speak to the nations (Note how they spoke in Gentile tongues; vv. 5-11. This was in harmony with Jesus' promise in Acts 1:8.)
      2. When you are filled with the Spirit...
         a. you will speak in tongues as the Spirit enables.
         b. you should be reminded of the purpose of your being filled with the Spirit—so you can become Christ's Spirit-empowered witness at home and "to the ends of the earth" (Ac 1:8).
   B. Next, Peter stood and *spoke by the Spirit a second time* (v. 14).
      1. But this time he did not speak in tongues.
         a. He spoke in the common language of the people.
         b. And yet, he was speaking by the Spirit every bit as much as when he earlier spoke in tongues.

2. Note: The word translated *"addressed* the crowd" in v. 14 is the same word translated "began to *"speak"* in v. 4.
   a. Peter was again speaking "as the Spirit enabled."
   b. He had become Christ's Spirit-empowered witness in fulfillment of Christ's promise in Acts 1:8.
3. God wants to do the same in your life.
   a. He wants to fill you with the Spirit.
   b. He wants you to speak in tongues.
   c. But most of all, He wants you to become His Spirit-empowered witness.

II. **WHILE WE OFTEN SPEAK OF THE FIRST KIND OF SPEAKING AS THE SPIRIT INSPIRES, WE SELDOM HEAR OF THE SECOND.**
   A. This has resulted in a tragic state of affairs.
      1. Our churches are full of Christians who often speak in tongues, yet seldom tell anyone about Jesus.
      2. The early believers could have never imagined such a thing.
   B. We must recapture the true meaning and purpose of Spirit baptism.
      1. Its purpose is empowerment for witness (Ac 1:8).
      2. A survey of the book of Acts reveals that being filled with the Spirit results in the following:
         a. A tremendous zeal to preach Christ to the lost.
         b. Boldness to witness for Christ in the face of danger.
         c. Divine guidance.
         d. Spirit-inspired, Spirit-directed speech.

III. **WHAT, THEN, MUST WE DO ABOUT THESE TRUTHS?**
   A. We must each be filled and re-filled with the Holy Spirit.
      1. This is the will of God for every believer (Eph 5:18).
   B. We should expect to speak in tongues when we are filled.
      1. This is the normative biblical sign.
      2. It brings a tremendous spiritual release.
   C. We must further expect to become Christ's Spirit-inspired witnesses.
      1. This is the calling of every believer (Lk 24:48).
      2. It is the purpose and expected result of Spirit-baptism.

Conclusion and Altar Call
Come now to be filled with the Spirit and become Christ's Spirit-empowered witness.

[DRM]

65. We Must Maintain a Missional Mindset

Sermon in a Sentence: We must remain focused on God's mission and the purpose for which God has raised us up.
Sermon Purpose: To see people empowered by the Spirit and focused on God's priority of winning the lost.
Text: Acts 6:1-5a; 8:1-5, 26-29, 39-40; 21:8-9

Introduction
1. Africa has many needs which we must not ignore, yet, we must not lose sight of God's priority.
2. Like the New Testament church, we must stay focused on the mission of God.
3. The life and ministry of Philip teaches us some important lessons that will help us maintain a missional mindset:

I. **LIKE PHILIP, WE MUST REMAIN MISSIONALY FOCUSED, EVEN WHEN ASKED TO SERVE IN HUMBLE POSITIONS** (Ac 6:1-5).
   A. Philip had a humble beginning.
      1. He accepted the humble task of being a "servant."
      2. And he was faithful to serve God where he was asked.
      3. The apostles needed people like Philip to serve so that they could remain focused on preaching the gospel (Ac 6:3-4).
   B. For some it would be humbling to be asked to serve in the way that Philip served.
      1. Yet, we should not despise the day of small beginnings.
      2. Philip was a man full of the Holy Spirit and faith; it would have been easy for him to argue that he was meant for bigger and better things.
      3. Nevertheless he stayed focused on the mission and not the advancement of his own personal agenda.
      4. He was a man who was full of the Spirit and wisdom (Ac 6:3).

II. **LIKE PHILIP, WE MUST REMAIN MISSIONALY FOCUSED, EVEN WHEN CIRCUMSTANCES MOVE US TO NEW PLACES** (Ac 8:1-5).
   A. When persecution broke out against the church, those who were scattered "preached Christ everywhere they went" (Ac 8:4).
      1. Philip is one of those who fled for their lives; however, he remained missionally-focused (Ac 8:5).

2. Africa is a continent on the run.
  3. We Africans understand what it means to be persecuted.
  B. Nevertheless, if we will maintain a missional mindset, we will preach Jesus wherever we go.
     1. It is easy to focus on the evil you are running from, but the church in Acts stayed focused on God's mission.
     2. If we will maintain a missional mindset, Africa's movement around the world will bring blessing to the nations.
     3. We must intentionally work to plant this missional mindset into our people.

III. **LIKE PHILIP, WE MUST REMAIN MISSIONALY FOCUSED, ESPECIALLY WHEN THE HOLY SPIRIT SUPERNATURALLY LEADS US** (Ac 8:26-29, 39-40).
   A. Philip was supernaturally led from a revival in Samaria to go and preach to one man on a desert road (Ac 8:26-29).
   B. In the natural this does not make sense.
   C. If we are to be God's missionary people, we must be ready to go anywhere the Spirit directs, even if the transition is painful.
      1. Philip followed the Spirit without knowing the whole plan.
      2. We must be willing to be led in the same way.

IV. **LIKE PHILIP, WE MUST LEAVE A LEGACY OF A MISSIONAL FOCUS FOR THE NEXT GENERATION** (Ac 21:8-9).
   A. It is significant that Philip had four daughters who were filled with the Spirit and involved in prophetic ministry (Ac 21:9).
   B. If God's mission is to go forward we must insure that the next generation is also focused on the mission.
   C. One key to creating a missional legacy for the next generation is to see an outpouring of the Spirit on the church, one that will include the youth and children.

Conclusion and Altar Call
   1. Let us determine today to stay focused on the mission of God.
   2. And let us come and seek a fresh outpouring of the Spirit on us for that purpose.

[LC]

66. Why the Spirit Came

Sermon in a Sentence: The Spirit has come to fill us with power and enable us to fulfill the Great Commission.

Sermon Purpose: To see people filled with the Spirit and empowered as witnesses.

Text: Acts 1:1-8

Introduction
1. In our text the disciples faced a great challenge; they were to be Christ's witnesses to the ends of the earth, but in themselves they were inadequate for the task.
2. We are in the same situation as they were.
3. Let us examine some of the reasons for the coming of the Spirit and discover how we, like the early disciples, can be successful:

I. THE HOLY SPIRIT HAS COME TO ENABLE US TO THINK GOD'S THOUGHTS (1Co 2:10-12).
A. God and man think differently (1Co 2:14, Isa 55:9).
B. Christ's discussion with His disciples shows this (Ac 1:6-8).
   1. The disciples' interests were different than Jesus'.
   2. They were thinking of reigning in Jerusalem; Christ was planning for them to be witnesses to the whole world.
C. This is why the Holy Spirit must come.
   1. Natural thinking is self-centered; God thinks of others.
   2. Something must take place to transform our thinking.
   3. The Spirit's coming accomplishes this (Jn 16:13-14).
   4. ILLUS: Because Peter was filled with the Spirit, he was able to receive God's thoughts, and he went to Cornelius house and salvation came to the Gentiles (Acts 10).
D. Once again we are in dire need of thinking God's thoughts.
   1. Much of the church today is focused on self-centered, human thinking.
   2. Pentecost has become a message of personal blessing rather than power for witness.
   3. The message of salvation is no longer focused on Christ but on social and economic revolution.
   4. God's program is not man's program. He has His own answers for the world's problems.
   5. We must listen to and partner with Him.

II. THE HOLY SPIRIT CAME TO ENABLE US TO SHARE GOD'S EMOTIONS (Ro 5:5-8).
A. Man loves himself and his friends who contribute to his happiness and personal desires.

  1. God is love, and He loves man with an unselfish love.
  2. He loved us even when we were sinners (Ro 5:6-8).
 B. Only God's Spirit can put that kind of love in us (Ro 5:5).
  1. Natural man will not love the lost and be willing to sacrifice and give himself to save them.
  2. The Holy Spirit comes to help us break through our psychological and emotional barriers and limitations to enlarge our hearts and make us channels of His love.

III. THE SPIRIT HAS COME TO ENABLE US TO PRAY GOD'S PRAYERS (Ro 8:26-27).

 A. We are limited in our ability to pray (Ro 8:26).
 B. The Spirit helps us to pray, giving us direct access to God (Ro 8:26-27, Eph 2:18).
  1. This is one important aspect of prayer in tongues.
  2. Paul stated that when we pray in an unknown tongue, our spirits pray (1Co 14:14).
 C. For the gospel to be proclaimed, and the world saved, we need the Spirit to help us to pray.
  1. Paul asked the church in Ephesus to pray for him in the Spirit so he would effectively proclaim the Gospel (Eph 6:18-20).

IV. THE HOLY SPIRIT CAME TO ENABLE US TO DO GOD'S WORK (Ac 1:8).

 A. God has always worked by His Spirit (Zec 4:6).
  1. This means we must not depend on anything more than we depend on God to work by the power of His Spirit.
 B. God bypasses the wisdom and might of this world and works through His anointed servants.
  1. The task is too great and the obstacles are too formidable to be met in mere human wisdom or strength.
  2 God changed a weak and inadequate minority into a mighty force when He filled the disciples with His Spirit.
 C. God has always led His people to victory in the face of overwhelming obstacles and He will do it again.
  1. He is looking for a people whom He can fill with His Spirit and empower to do His work.

Conclusion and Altar Call
Come now and seek to be filled with the Spirit and become a powerful witness for Jesus Christ.

[MH]

---

* Editor's Note: This sermon outline is adapted from an article by the same name by Melvin L. Hodges appearing in *Paraclete,* Winter 1970.

67. Your Daughters Shall Prophesy

Sermon in a Sentence: Women can be filled with the Spirit and used by God as His Spirit-empowered witnesses.

Sermon Purpose: That women will be filled with the Spirit, and that they will know that God can powerfully use them to advance His kingdom.

Text: Acts 2:17-18; 21:8-9

Introduction
1. God gives the Holy Spirit to women just as He does to men.
   a. "Your … daughters shall prophesy" (Ac 2:17).
   b. Philip had four daughters who prophesied (Ac 21:9).
   c. Women were present on the Day of Pentecost and were filled with the Spirit (Ac 1:14; 2:4).
2. God gives His Spirit to women for the same reason He gives the Spirit to men: to empower them as His witnesses (Ac 1:8).
3. This message will discuss how women can be filled with the Spirit and used by God to advance the kingdom of God.

I. FIVE THINGS EVERY WOMAN SHOULD KNOW ABOUT RECEIVING THE HOLY SPIRIT:
   A. First, every woman needs the Holy Spirit (Eph 5:18).
   B. Second, the Heavenly Father is ready to give the Spirit to any woman who will ask (Lk 11:13).
   C. Third, women must hunger and thirst for the Spirit (Mt 5:6; Jn 7:37-38).
   D. Fourth, it is easy to be filled with the Spirit. (In fact, it is as easy as breathing [Jn 20:21-22]).
   E. Fifth, God will powerfully use any woman who will be filled with the Holy Spirit and obey the command of Christ to preach the gospel (Lk 24:45-48).

II. THE ONE THING EVERY WOMAN NEEDS TO RECEIVE THE SPIRIT—*FAITH*
   A. Jesus said, "*Whoever believes* in me, as the Scripture has said, streams of living water will flow from within him" (Jn 7:38).
   B. In Galatians 3 Paul taught that …
      1. … "you receive the Spirit *by… believing*" (v. 2).
      2. … "God gave you his Spirit *because you believed*" (v. 5).
      3. … *"by faith* we … receive the promise of the Spirit." (v. 14)

III. **THREE FAITH-STEPS EVERY WOMAN CAN TAKE TO RECEIVE THE HOLY SPIRIT TODAY:**
   A. Ask in Faith.
      1. Jesus promised, "Ask and it will be given you." (Lk 11:9).
      2. Further, He said, "How much more will your Father give the Holy Spirit to those who ask Him." (Lk 11:13).
   B. Receive by Faith.
      1. Jesus promised, "For everyone who asks receives" (Lk 11:10).
      2. He further promised, "Therefore I tell you, whatever you ask for in prayer, believe that you have received it, and it will be yours." (Mk 11:24).
   C. Speak in Faith.
      1. On the Day of Pentecost, "They were all filled with the Spirit *and began to speak.*" (Ac 2:4).
      2. Jesus said, "Whoever believes in me, as the Scripture has said, streams of living water will flow from within him." (Jn 7:38).

IV. **ONE THING A WOMAN MUST DO ONCE SHE HAS RECEIVED THE HOLY SPIRIT:**
   A. Every woman must be a witness for Christ (Ac 1:8).
   B. The same Spirit who anoints women to speak in tongues also anoints them to tell others about Jesus.

Conclusion and Altar Call
   Come and be filled with the Holy Spirit today.

[DRM]

SECTION 3

LIFE IN THE SPIRIT

68. Eight Reasons You Should Be Praying In Tongues

Sermon in a Sentence: There are many positive reasons believers should pray in tongues every day.
Sermon Purpose: That believers will be baptized in the Spirit and utilize the gift of tongues in private devotion and public worship.
Text: 1 Corinthians 14:18

Introduction
1. Pentecostals are distinguished by many things (such as zeal, worship, preaching). One of those things is speaking in tongues.
2. Some have asked, "Why do Pentecostals emphasize speaking in tongues? What good is it?"
3. Here are eight reasons you should be praying in tongues everyday:

I. BECAUSE SPEAKING IN TONGUES IS THE BIBLICAL SIGN OF BEING BAPTIZED IN THE HOLY SPIRIT.
   A. It is the recurring sign in Acts (Ac 2:4; 10:46; 19:6).
   B. When you are baptized in the Holy Spirit, you will know.
      1. Don't be cheated out of the real thing!
      2. **ILLUS**: Someone asked, "Do I have to speak in tongues to be filled with the Spirit." The preacher answered, "You are asking the wrong question. The right question is, 'Do I get to speak in tongues?' Speaking in tongues is a wonderful privilege of every Spirit-filled believer."

II. BECAUSE PRAYING IN TONGUES BUILDS YOU UP SPIRITUALLY (1Co 14:4).
   A. Like our physical bodies, our spirit need exercise.
   B. One form of spiritual exercise is praying in tongues.

III. BECAUSE SPEAKING IN TONGUES IS A POWERFUL, GOD-GIVEN MEANS OF INTERCESSORY PRAYER (Ro 8:26-27).
   A. This text tells us four things about our prayer lives:
      1. We don't know how to pray as we should.
      2. The Spirit will help us to pray.
      3. The Holy Spirit will pray through us with "groans that words cannot express" (NIV).
      4. He will pray through us "according to the will of God."
   B. Here is how it works:
      1. You begin to pray, allowing the Spirit to take over.
      2. Sometimes there are needs you don't know about.

3. Sometimes there are needs that you know about, but you don't know how to pray for them.
4. Yield to the Spirit and allow Him pray through you!

IV. **BECAUSE PRAYING IN TONGUES CREATES AN AWARENESS OF GOD'S INDWELLING PRESENCE.**
   A. The Bible gives us wonderful promises of God's presence:
      1. Such as Mt 28:20; Ac 17:27-28; and Heb 13:5.
      2. And yet, sometimes God seems so distant.
   B. Praying in tongues is a wonderful remedy for this problem.

V. **BECAUSE PRAYING IN TONGUES WILL BUILD YOUR FAITH** (Jude 20).
   A. The Bible speaks of ways we can build up our faith:
      1. Through reading and practicing the Word of God.
      2. By exercising the faith that we have.
   B. One oft-neglected way is praying in tongues (Jude 20).

VI. **BECAUSE PRAYING IN TONGUES IS A WAY TO WRAP YOURSELF IN THE LOVE OF GOD** (Jude 20-21; Ro 5:5).
   A. We sing, "Jesus loves me this I know, because the Bible tells me so."
      1. And it is true—whether I feel it or not!
      2. But oh, how wonderful to experience the love of God.
   B. Prayer in the Spirit helps us keep ourselves in God's love.

VII. **BECAUSE, TOGETHER WITH THE GIFT OF INTERPRETATION, IT IS ONE WAY GOD COMMUNICATES A PROPHETIC WORD TO HIS CHURCH** (1Co 14:5).
   A. Sometimes God wants to speak directly to a congregation through the gifts of tongues and interpretation.
   B. At such times the church is edified and built up.

VIII. **BECAUSE PRAYING IN TONGUES PROVIDES A PERFECT CHANNEL FOR JOYOUS PRAISE AND WORSHIP** (Jn 4:24).
   A. Have you ever been so filled with joy and gratitude that you could find no words to express that joy?
   B. Prayer and praise in tongues is a perfect means to express that joy and gratitude.

Conclusion and Altar Call
1. Is it any wonder why Paul said, "I thank my God that I speak in tongues more than you all" (1Co 14:18).
2. Come now to be filled with the Spirit.

[DRM]

69. The Fire, the Wind, and the Dove

Sermon in a Sentence: Like fire, wind, and the dove, the Holy Spirit will purge us of our sin, lead us into truth, bring us into unity, drive us into the harvest, and call us into a closer walk with God.
Sermon Purpose: That believers might be filled with the Spirit and understand the Spirit's work in their lives.
Text: Luke 11:11-13

Introduction
1. In our text Jesus tells us that we should not be afraid to allow the Holy Spirit to work in our lives.
2. This is true because…
   a. … God will not give to us something harmful to us (like a stone snake, or a scorpion).
   b. … God will only give us things that are beneficial to us (like bread, a fish, or an egg).
   c. … the Holy Spirit gives to us Jesus, the Bread of Life, the One who gives life to the world.
3. In doing this, the Spirit will come to us in three ways: as fire, as wind, and as a dove.

I. THE HOLY SPIRIT COMES LIKE A DEVOURING FIRE.
A. In Scripture the Holy Spirit is sometimes depicted as a fire or a flame.
   1. This is seen in John's prediction of Jesus (Lk 3:16).
   2. This is also shown in the flame of Pentecost (Ac 2:3).
B. Like fire, when the Holy Spirit comes, He changes us and we are no longer the same.
   1. The Spirit convicts us of our sins (Jn 16:8-11).
      a. Like on the Day of Pentecost (Ac 2:37).
   2. The Spirit leads us in the path of divine truth.
      a. He is the Spirit of Truth (Jn 14:7; 15:26; 16:13).
      b. He reveals to us that Jesus is the way, the truth and the life (Jn 14:6).
   3. The Spirit brings revival to us and the church.

II. THE HOLY SPIRIT MOVES LIKE AN IMPETUOUS WIND.
A. The Spirit came as a powerful wind at Pentecost (Ac 2:2).
B. Like a powerful wind, the Spirit destroys all human barriers that hinder us from becoming one body in Christ.
   1. Every nation has its own prejudices, customs, and traditions that cause division.
   2. For instance, the Jews believed that they had a monopoly on God, but the Spirit showed Peter and the

Jewish Christians in Jerusalem that God is the God of all peoples and nations (Ac 10:1-46).
   3. Only the Holy Spirit can unite all people and remove all of the ethnic barriers that separate them.
C. Like a wind, the Spirit will drive us into the harvest.
   1. The Spirit sent out Barnabas and Saul (Ac 13:1-4).
   2. The Spirit will empower us to spread the knowledge of Jesus throughout the world so that all men can be saved (Ac 1:8).

III. THE HOLY SPIRIT DESCENDS LIKE A GENTLE DOVE.
A. The Spirit descended upon Jesus as a dove (Lk 2:22-23).
B. The dove is a gentle creature.
   1. For Noah the dove was a sign that the water had decreased on the surface of the earth, and that soon a new earth would appear, an earth washed from its sin and violence (Ge 8:8-12).
   2. The Spirit's coming on Jesus as a dove was a sign that Jesus was bringing the hope of a new world (Lk 3:22; Ro 5:4-5).
C. Sometimes the Spirit will come to us as a soft whisper, directing us and drawing us close to God.
   1. As He did with Elijah (1Kg 9:19).
   2. As Jesus did with Peter (Jn 21:15-17).

Conclusion and Altar Call
   1. The Spirit will come to you like a devouring fire, an impetuous wind, and a gentle dove.
   2. Come now and be filled with the Spirit.

[NB }

70. Getting to Know Our Leader

Sermon in a Sentence: The Holy Spirit is more than a spiritual force to be manipulated or a tool to be used by Christians; He is a divine Person who wants to indwell and empower believers for service.

Sermon Purpose: That believers will come to know the power and presence of the Holy Spirit by being baptized in the Spirit.

Texts: John 14:16; 15:26; 16:7-8

Introduction
1. One of our primary responsibilities as believers is to follow the leadership of the Holy Spirit.
2. However, before we can properly follow the leading of the Spirit, we must first get to know Him as a person.
3. This message will help us get to know our Leader, the Holy Spirit.

I. **WHO IS THE HOLY SPIRIT?**
   A. People think about the Holy Spirit in different ways.
      1. As a mysterious force, like wind or gravity.
      2. As an energy force to be harnessed and used, like electricity, or even witchcraft.
   B. According to the Bible the Holy Spirit is a Person.
      1. Therefore, He is not something I can "get hold of" to use for my own personal benefit.
      2. He is rather a divine Person who lives in me to enable me to do the will of God.
      3. As a Person, the Spirit wants a living relationship with each of us.
   C. What the church needs today is not better programs or equipment, but a deeper relationship with the Holy Spirit.
      1. Only He can give life to the church.
      2. Illustration: A new program for a dead church is like a heart pacemaker for a dead patient.

II. **HOW DOES THE HOLY SPIRIT FIT INTO THE GODHEAD?**
   A. God the Father is the Creator.
      1. From Him we get a sense of belonging.
      2. Because He created us, we belong to Him.
   B. God the Son is the Savior.
      1. From Him we get our sense of worth.
      2. Because He died for us, we are valuable.
   C. God the Spirit is the personal presence of God today.
      1. From Him we get a sense of confidence.

2. Because He is with us, we are not alone.

III. WHAT DID JESUS SAY ABOUT THE HOLY SPIRIT?
(Note: He said many things; however, we will center our thoughts on what He said in our texts. In these texts Jesus referred to the Spirit in two ways)
  A. Jesus called the Holy Spirit the "Counselor" (Jn 14:16).
   1. The word translated "Counselor" (*Gk. Parakletos*) literally means "one who is called along side to assist."
   2. The Holy Spirit does not work in spite of us, or instead of us, but with us and through us.
   3. In working with us the Spirit will do two things:
      a. He will convict us and bring to light the sin in our lives (Jn 16:7-8).
      b. He will train us to be all that God wants us to be.
   4. Application: The Spirit will also speak through Spirit-filled believers to bring conviction to the lost—just as He did through Peter on the Day of Pentecost (Ac 2:14ff; 37-41)
   5. The real value of being led by the Spirit is not primarily what happens inside the church but what happens out there in the world.
  B. Jesus called the Holy Spirit our "Guide."
   1. As the Spirit of Truth, He will guide us into all truth (Jn 16:13).
   2. Life is too tough to navigate without our Guide.
   3. Submit yourself to Him, and He will guide you.

Conclusion and Altar Call
  1. You can deepen your relationship with the Lord by being filled with the Spirit today.
  2. You can also become an effective witness for Him.
  3. Come now to be filled and refilled with the Spirit.

[DJ]

71 The Gift of Tongues

Sermon in a Sentence: The gift of tongues is often misunderstood, and many miss the spiritual blessing it can bring to their lives.
Sermon Purpose: To help believers accept that God wants to fill them with His Holy Spirit and give them the gift of tongues.
Text: 1 Corinthians 12:8-11

Introduction
1. For New Testament Christians speaking in tongues was a normal practice.
2. In this message we will consider the biblical answer to three questions about the gift of tongues:

I. **WHAT IS SPEAKING IN TONGUES?**
   A. First, what speaking in tongues *is not:*.
      1. It is not gibberish, babble or baby talk (Ac 2:5,6,8,11).
         a. Tongues = language of men or angels (1Co 13:2).
      2. It is not ecstatic speech or a trance-like state.
         a. You are in control of your mind (1Co 14:27-33).
      3. It is not a gift that ended with the apostolic age.
         a. 1Co 13:8 is often misinterpreted.
         b. It refers to things that will change in the age to come when Christ returns.
      4. It is not a spiritual gift that embarrassed Paul.
         a. In 1Cor 12-14 Paul is not trying to explain away something he was embarrassed about. He is rather correcting abuses in the church.
         b. He was no more embarrassed by tongues than he was of the Lord's Supper when he corrected abuses of it in chapter 11.
         c. Neither should we be embarrassed. Tongues is a gift from God, and God only gives good gifts.
   B. What speaking in tongues *is:*
      1. It is Spirit-inspired speech (Ac 2:4).
      2. It is declaring the wonderful works of God (Ac 2:11).
      3. It is speaking to God (1Co 14:2).
      4. It is Spirit-prompted prayer (1Co 14:15-16, Ro 8:26-27).
      5. It is Spirit-directed praise and thanksgiving (1Co 14:14).

II. **IS THIS AN EXPERIENCE FOR EVERY BELIEVER?**
   A. In terms of personal prayer, both Luke and Paul show that tongues are intended for all believers.
      1. At Pentecost all who were baptized in the Holy Spirit spoke in tongues (Ac 2:4).

2. At Cornelius' house all who were filled with the Spirit spoke in tongues (Ac 10:44-46).
   3. Paul thanked God that he spoke in tongues and wished that everyone spoke in tongues (1Co 14:5,18).
   4. Paul taught that tongues are given so that believers can build themselves up in prayer (1Co 14:4).
      a. The Spirit is the Christian's best counselor.
      b. The Lord has given us this gift to strengthen us and minister to our spirits.
   B. However, tongues, as a spiritual gift intended for public use, is not for all believers.
      1. When Paul asks, "Do all speak in tongues?" (1Co. 12:29) he is referring to the public exercise of the gift of tongues accompanied by interpretation, the purpose of which is to edify the church.

III. **WHAT GUIDELINES ARE WE TO FOLLOW FOR THE PUBLIC USE OF TONGUES?**
   A. In our church services we should encourage this manifestation of the Spirit.
      1. Paul wrote, "Desire spiritual gifts and do not forbid speaking in tongues" (1Co 14:1, 39).
      2. Thus, we should encourage the use of this gift with scriptural guidelines (1Co 14:33, 40).
   B. When exercised publicly, the gift of tongues should be accompanied by the gift of interpretation so the entire church can be strengthened (1Co 14:4-6, 13, 28).
   C. The gift of tongues with interpretation should be limited to two or three messages for each worship service (1Co 14:26-27).
   D. The key to all the speaking gifts (tongues, interpretation, prophecy) is prayer accompanied by faith.

Conclusion and Altar Call
   1. We should all desire all that God wants for us.
   2. Come to God now and allow His Spirit to fill you and pray through you.

[GW]

72. The Helper

Sermon in a Sentence: If we will be filled with the Holy Spirit, He will help us to live effective Christian lives.

Sermon Purpose: That believers be filled with the Holy Spirit and become more effective Christians.

Text: John 14:16 (NKJV)

Introduction
1. The Holy Spirit has been given a "bad name" in society today—and it is partly our fault.
    a. Because we seek His power more than His person.
    b. Because we want more from God than we want of God.
    c. Because we want His gifts more than we want His fruit.
    d. Because we want the Spirit to perform rather than surrendering our lives to Him.
    e. Because we Pentecostals have used the Holy Spirit as a badge of superiority rather than submitting ourselves to Him and His will.
2. When we do these things we become, what Paul called, "a resounding gong or a clanging cymbal" (1Co 13:1).
3. In our text Jesus describes the Holy Spirit as "another Helper."
    a. In this "Upper Room Discourse" Jesus repeatedly talked about the Holy Spirit (i.e., Jn 14:15-21; 25-27; 15:26-27; 16:7-15).
    b. He revealed four reasons we need the Holy Spirit as our Helper:

I. **THE HOLY SPIRIT IS THE ONE WHO CONVICTS.**
   A. According to John 16:8-11 He convicts in three ways:
      1. He convicts of sin. (He says "No, no.")
      2. He convicts of righteousness. (He says, "Yes, yes.")
      3. He convicts of judgment. (He says, "You choose.")
   B. We can conquer sin through the power of the Holy Spirit (Ro 8:1-4; Gal 5:16).
      1. The Holy Spirit convicts us so that we might have a better life (Jn 10:10).
      2. His conviction leads us to eternal life.

II. **THE HOLY SPIRIT IS THE SPIRIT OF TRUTH** (Jn 14:17; 15:26; 16:13).
   A. Our society teaches us that sin okay.
      1. It presents lies as if they were truth.
      2. However, the Holy Spirit comes to us with the real truth.

- B. What happens when we live with the Spirit of Truth?
  1. He provides supernatural liberty (Jn 8:32).
  2. We become powerful witnesses to the truth of the gospel (Ac 1:8).

III. THE HOLY SPIRIT IS OUR GUIDE (Jn 16:13).
- A. He will guide us into a more fruitful lives (Jn 15:5, 8).
- B. He will tell us where to go and who to witness to (Ac 10:19-20).
- C. He will provide courageous leadership for us and will take us places we have never gone before.
- D. We must obey and follow Him (Ac 5:32).

IV. THE HOLY SPIRIT IS OUR TEACHER.
- A. When the Holy Spirit comes, He teaches us (Jn 14:26).
- B. However, before He can teach us …
  1. … we must be willing to learn from Him.
  2. … we must humble ourselves and admit we need help.
- C. As our teacher the Holy Spirit …
  1. … provides priceless lessons.
  2. … teaches us things we have never learned before.

Conclusion and Altar Call
1. A relationship with the Spirit begins with a relationship with Jesus Christ (Jn 3:3-7).
2. Once we have been born again, we must then be filled with the Spirit (Eph 5:18).
3. Come now and receive Christ.
4. Come now and be filled with the Spirit.

[EJ]

73 In Step with the Spirit

Sermon in a Sentence: Once we have been baptized in the Holy Spirit we should then live a life "in step with the Spirit."
Sermon Purpose: That believers will be filled with the Spirit and committed to live a life in step with the Spirit.
Text: Galatians 5:25 (NIV)

Introduction
1. Soon after being born again, every believer should be baptized in the Holy Spirit.
2. This is the scriptural norm.
3. However, being filled with the Spirit is not an end in itself; it is the beginning of a life lived in step with the Spirit.
4. There are seven powerful principles about living in step with the Spirit that every believer should understand and apply:

I. A LIFE IN STEP WITH THE SPIRIT IS A LIFE OF PRAYER.
A. A Spirit-filled life begins with prayer.
   1. We must ask for the Spirit (Lk 11:9-13).
   2. Before Pentecost the people prayed (Ac 1:1 4 with 2:4).
B. A Spirit-filled life is sustained by prayer.
   1. Prayer is for the Spirit-filled life what breathing is for our natural lives (Jn 20:22).

II. A LIFE IN STEP WITH THE SPIRIT IS A LIFE OF HOLINESS.
A. Unholy living will grieve the Holy Spirit (Eph 4:30-31).
B. The Spirit will empower us to live holy lives (Ro 8:1-2; Ga 5:16).

III. A LIFE IN STEP WITH THE SPIRIT IS A LIFE OF FAITH.
A. It is a life of faith from first until last.
   1. It begins in faith (Jn 7:38; Gal 3:14).
   2. It is sustained by faith.
B. Our faith is built up through prayer in the Spirit (Jude 20).

IV. A LIFE IN STEP WITH THE SPIRIT IS A LIFE OF SPIRITUAL GROWTH AND CONTINUALLY DEEPENING RELATIONSHIPS.
A. Once we have been filled with the Spirit we must mature in the things of the Spirit.
   1. In the gifts of the Spirit (1Co 12:1, 31).
   2. In the fruit of the Spirit (Gal 5:22-23).
B. Life in the Spirit also involves continually deepening relationships.

1. With the Father, the Son, and the Holy Spirit.
2. With other believers in Christ.
3. With those who need Christ.
- C. Like any relationship, our relationship with God must be nourished and maintained.

V. A LIFE IN STEP WITH THE SPIRIT IS A LIFE OF BOLD WITNESS.
- A. Power for witness is the primary purpose of Spirit baptism (Ac 1:8; 4:31).
- B. If we will take the initiative, and begin to witness, the Spirit will come and energize our witness.

VI. A LIFE IN STEP WITH THE SPIRIT BEGINS WITH TWO POWERFUL SPIRITUAL EXPERIENCES—AND IT IS SUSTAINED BY MANY SUBSEQUENT SPIRITUAL EXPERIENCES.
- A. Life in the Spirit begins with two powerful experiences:
    1. The new birth (Jn 3:3-7).
    2. The baptism in the Holy Spirit (Ac 2:1-4).
- B. It is sustained by many subsequent experiences, including
    1. Refillings (Ac 4:31; Eph 5:18).
    2. Anointings (Ac 4:8; 10:38).
    3. Divine guidance (Ac 16:6-10).

Conclusion and Altar Call
1. Come and be born of the Spirit.
2. Come and be filled with the Holy Spirit.
3. Come and commit yourself to a life lived in step with the Spirit.

[DRM]

74. Life in the Spirit

Sermon in a Sentence: It is not enough to have only the power of the Spirit, we must also have the purity of the Spirit in our lives.
Sermon Purpose: To see people filled with the Spirit and begin to daily walk in the Spirit as holy children of God.
Text: Romans 8:1-39

Introduction
1. True Pentecostalism emphasizes both power and purity.
2. The Holy Spirit is both "Holy" and "Spirit."
   a. The *Holy* of His name reminds us of His sanctifying work in the life of the believer; the *Spirit* of His name reminds us of His empowering work in the life of the believer.
   b. The *Holy* reminds us that we are to conform to Christ's image. The *Spirit* reminds us we are to continue His work.
3. The Christian's struggle is between the flesh and the spirit.
   a. Paul addressed this struggle in Romans 7-8.
   b. Chapter 7 shows the strong side of the flesh.
   c. Chapter 8 shows the Christian's victory over the flesh by the blood of Jesus and the power of the Holy Spirit.
4. Romans 8:1 describes past action that took place at a definite moment.
   a. This action is Christ's work at Calvary (Ga 5:1).
   b. This work is foundational to our present freedom in Christ.
5. In this message we will look at a life lived in the Spirit.
6. Such a life in the Spirit has two main characteristics:

I. **LIFE IN THE SPIRIT IS A LIFE OF HOLINESS** (Ro 8:5-13).
   A. We must first crucify the flesh (Ga 5:16-21).
      1. The believer should walk in the Spirit, not the flesh.
         a. To walk in (or by) the Spirit is to submit to the Spirit.
         b. It is to remain in communion with Him and make decisions in the light of His nature.
      2. We cannot be occupied sin with and Christ at the same time.
      3. The believer's responsibility is to yield to the Spirit and to resist the works of the flesh.
   B. Then we must cultivate the Spirit (Ga 5:22-25).
      1. Paul distinguishes between the works of the flesh, and the fruit of the Spirit (Ga 5:22-23).
      2. Works are produced by human energy; fruit is grown as a branch abides in the vine (Jn 15:5).
      3. Note that the word "fruit" is singular. The one kind of fruit the Spirit produces is Christlikeness.

II. LIFE IN THE SPIRIT IS A LIFE OF POWER (Ro 8:14-30).
   A. The Spirit gives us power to be God's children (vv 14-16).
      1. He continually gives us assurance we belong to Him.
         a. He has taken care of our past, present, and future.
         b. There should be no doubt that we are God's children
      2. He is the agent and aid who bears witness and confirms to us that we are God's children.
      3. Note the double testimony in these verses:
         a. We have God's testimony that He alone is the one who has adopted us into His family.
         b. Now we each have our own experience with the Spirit. ("His Spirit lets us know.") We are now His special children!
   B. The Spirit gives us power to pray (Ro 8:26-27).
      1. He will help us when we cannot help ourselves.
      2. He will help bear the burdens of our lives.
      3. He will help us to pray.
   C. The Spirit gives us power for purpose (Ro 8:28-30).
      1. He gives us power to fulfill our destinies (Ro 8:29-39)
      2. God has destined each of us for a glorious end!

Conclusion and Altar Call
   1. Through the Spirit we can live lives of holiness and power.
   2. Come now and surrender your life to the Holy Spirit.
   3. Come and be empowered by Him to do His work.

[SE]

75 | Living by the Nudge

Sermon in a Sentence: We must each know how to "live by the nudge," that is, to walk in the Spirit.
Sermon Purpose: That believers be filled with the Spirit and commit themselves to living in the Spirit.
Text: Romans 8:1-17

Introduction
1. The work of Holy Spirit must be a priority in each of our lives (Gal 5:25).
2. This message will discuss what it means to live and walk in the Spirit.
3. In our text Paul challenges us to live our lives "according to the Spirit." First, he discusses…

I. TWO WAYS WE MAY LIVE OUR CHRISTIAN LIVES.
   1. We can live them "according to the sinful nature" [Gk. *kata sarka*]
   2. Or we can live them "according to the Spirit" [Gk. *kata Pneuma*, vv. 4-5]). Let's look at each way:
   A. We can live our lives *kata sarka*, that is, according to the sinful nature ("according to the flesh," vv 1-4, 7).
      1. Such a life cannot please God.
      2. It results in selfishness, hostility and resistance to God.
      3. It leads to slavery and death.
      4. There is a better way:
   B. We can live our lives *kata Pneuma*, that is, according to the Spirit.
      1. Living *kata Pneuma* results in a life of righteousness, peace, and freedom from condemnation.
      2. No matter what our background (legalistic or pagan), we can live righteously through the power of the Spirit.

II. HOW WE CAN LIVE OUR LIVES ACCORDING TO THE SPIRIT.
   A. We must begin by being born of the Spirit (Jn 3:3-8).
   B. Next, we must have the correct view of the Holy Spirit.
      1. We must not view Him as a passive, hidden influence in our lives.
      2. Neither must we view Him as only occasionally working in us (as in times of revival).
      3. We must, rather, view the Spirit is an active dynamic Person working in our lives at all times.

- C. Further, we must learn to "live by the nudge."
    1. The "nudge" is the sensitive and significant impression of the Holy Spirit deep within our lives that motivates us to speak, serve, and act according to the redemptive purposes of God.
    2. It is the secret of a victorious Christian life.
    3. It is the secret of a powerful Christian witness.
- D. To live by the nudge is to live a life sensitive and responsive to the Holy Spirit in three contexts:
    1. In the context of *our own personal Christian lives:*
       He will nudge us and move us into greater effectiveness, maturity, and victory over sin.
    2. In the context of *the church gathered for worship:*
       He will nudge us to minister to one another.
    3. In *the context of the marketplace:*
       He nudges us to reach out to the lost with the gospel.
- E. You ask, "How then can I live my life *kata Pneuma?*" (Seven practical suggestions:)
    1. Recognize the Holy Spirit's presence in your life.
    2. Realize that the Spirit is all around you working in and through the circumstances of your life.
    3. Get rid of your need to be noticed by others.
    4. Start each day in prayer, asking the Spirit to come, lead, and use you.
    5. Be constantly sensitive to the Spirit's nudge.
    6. Seek to be a blessing to others.
    7. Reflect on how well you have responded to the Spirit in the past, then adjust your life and response in order to more effectively respond to Him in the future.

Conclusion and Altar Call
1. Are you ready to live your life in step with the Spirit?
2. Come now and commit yourself to pursuing the Spirit-directed life.
3. Begin by being filled and refilled with the Holy Spirit today.

[LB]

76. Now That You Have Been Filled with the Spirit

Sermon in a Sentence: Once a person has been filled with the Spirit, he or she must maintain the Spirit-filled walk, witness for Christ, and grow in grace.

Sermon Purpose: That believers be filled with the Spirit and learn how to live the Spirit-filled life.

Texts: Galatians 3:2-3; 5:25

Introduction
1. It is vital that every believer be baptized in the Holy Spirit.
2. But there is a problem: Many times, once Christians have been filled with the Spirit, they don't know how to live the Spirit-controlled life.
3. Our texts talk about the importance of living our Christian lives under the control of the Holy Spirit.
4. This message will discuss four things you must do once you have been filled with the Spirit:

Now that you have been filled with the Spirit…
I. **YOU SHOULD REMAIN FULL OF THE SPIRIT.**
   A. You must seek fresh infillings of the Spirit.
      1. Being filled with the Spirit is not a one-time-only experience. (Compare Ac 2:4; 4:8, 31.) (Compare Ac 9:6, Eph 5:18.)
      2. We must be refilled with the Spirit every day!
   B. Pray without ceasing (1Th 5:17).
      1. Prayer is a key element in maintaining the Spirit-filled life.
      2. Our prayer times should include prayer in the Spirit (Eph 6:18).
   C. Live a holy life.
      1. Unholy living will grieve the Spirit of God (Eph 4:3).
      2. Allow the Spirit to sanctify your life (Ro 15:16).
   D. Live a submitted life (Jas 4:17-18).
      1. We must daily submit ourselves to God's will.
      2. We must daily commit ourselves to God's mission.

Now that you have been filled with the Spirit...
II. **YOU SHOULD BECOME A POWERFUL WITNESS FOR CHRIST.**
   A. Power for witness is the main reason we are filled with the Spirit (Ac 1:8).

    B. We are to faithfully tell others about Christ and what He can do in their lives (Lk 24:46-48; Ac 5:32).

Now that you have been filled with the Spirit...
III. YOU SHOULD BE USED BY GOD IN THE MINISTRY OF SPIRITUAL GIFTS.
    A. Since the gifts reside in the Spirit, when we are filled with the Spirit we are ready to be used in the ministry of spiritual gifts.
    B. A list of spiritual gifts is found in 1 Corinthians 12:8-10.
    C. The Spirit wants to use you:
        1. To speak to you (revelation gifts).
        2. To speak through you (prophetic gifts).
        3. To work through you (power gifts).
    D. We should each covet earnestly the gifts (1Co 14:1).

Now that you have been filled with the Spirit...
IV. YOU SHOULD ALLOW THE HOLY SPIRIT TO PRODUCE SPIRITUAL FRUIT IN YOUR LIFE.
    A. The fruit of the Spirit are produced in our lives as we...
        1. ... walk in the Spirit (Gal 5:22-35, note v. 25).
        2. ... abide in Christ (Jn 15:4-6).
    B. The nine fruit of the Spirit describe the character of Christ.
        1. Christ wants us to live as He lived (1Jn 2:6).
        2. We can only do this through the power of the Spirit.

Conclusion and Altar Call
    1. Come now to be filled or re-filled with the Spirit.
    2. As you do...
        a. Commit yourself to being Christ's Spirit-filled witness.
        b. Ask the Spirit to begin to release spiritual gifts in your life.
        c. Commit yourself to allowing the Spirit work in your life to produce spiritual fruit.

[DRM]

77 Obeying the Spirit's Voice

Sermon in a Sentence: We must all be filled with the Spirit and learn to obey the voice of the Spirit.

Sermon Purpose: That believers be filled with the Spirit and commit themselves to obeying His voice.

Texts: Acts 8:26-29

Introduction:
1. We must all be filled with the Holy Spirit, but that is not enough.
2. We must also learn how to obey the voice of the Spirit.
3. Our text is one of several examples in the book of Acts of believers obeying the voice of the Spirit.
4. Let's look at three of those examples:

I. **PHILIP OBEYED THE SPIRIT'S VOICE** (Ac 8:26-27).
   A. Philip heard and obeyed the Spirit's command two times:
      1. When the Spirit said, "Go" to the Gaza Road (v. 26).
      2. When the Spirit said, "Draw near to the chariot" (v. 29).
      3. Philip could hear the Spirit's voice because he was full of the Spirit and he had an obedient heart (Ac 6:1-6).
   B. Because Philip obeyed the Spirit's voice, he was successful.
      1. The Ethiopian found Christ (Ac 8:36-39).
      2. God fills us with His Spirit so we can hear His voice, obey, go, and effectively witness for Christ.

II. **ANANIAS OBEYED THE SPIRIT'S VOICE** (Ac 9:10-18).
   A. The Spirit told Ananias to go and pray for Saul.
      1. Ananias obeyed even though he was afraid.
      2. Read verses 11 and 15.
   B. As a result of his obedience a great work was done.
      1. Paul was filled with the Spirit and commissioned as the apostle to the Gentiles.
      2. As a result many came to Christ.
   C. We, too, must obey the Spirit's voice, even when it is hard.

III. **PETER OBEYED THE SPIRIT'S VOICE** (Ac 10:1-48).
   A. The Spirit directed Peter to "Go."
   B. Peter obeyed even though it brought him into conflict with his culture and religious traditions.
   C. Peter's obedience resulted in the opening of the door for the gospel to the Gentiles.

IV. WE, TOO, MUST OBEY THE SPIRIT'S VOICE.
  A. Like these three men, we must each be filled with the Spirit.
  B. Like these three men, we must each be obedient to the Spirit's voice.
      1. To be filled with the Spirit is to be obedient to the Spirit.
      2. If you will listen to the Spirit's voice, He will direct you into the mission of God.
  C. From these three men we learn some powerful spiritual lessons:
      1. We must all be filled with the Spirit (Ac 1:4-5, Eph 5:18).
      2. We must remain open to the Spirit's voice.
      3. We must obey the Spirit's voice, even when it is hard.
      4. When the Spirit directs us to someone, we can be assured that He has prepared the one to whom He directs us.
      5. If we will obey the Spirit's voice, powerful results will follow.

Conclusion and Altar Call
  1. Come now to be filled with the Spirit
  2. And commit yourself to hearing and obeying the Spirit's voice.

[BN]

78. Results of Authentic Pentecostalism

Sermon in a Sentence: In spite of some who have given Pentecostalism a bad name, there is an authentic Pentecostalism that transforms people and churches.

Sermon Purpose: To encourage people not to reject Pentecost due to abuses but rather to seek to be filled with the Spirit's power.

Text: Acts 2:1-4; 14-18

Introduction
1. Pentecostalism has received a bad reputation in some places...
    a. ... because of excesses which have been allowed.
    b. ... because of failure to demonstrate the power of Pentecost.
    c. ... because of legalism that has been championed.
    d. ... because of scammers with fraudulent intentions.
2. In spite of this, there is an authentic Pentecostalism which brings with it the ability for the church to rise to a level never before achieved.
3. Let's look at four evidences of authentic Pentecostalism:

I. **AUTHENTIC PENTECOSTALISM RAISES THE LEVEL OF A BELIEVER'S PRAYER LIFE.**
   A. Pentecostals have historically been known for their praying.
   B. Jesus, our great example, gave us a pattern for us to follow:
      1. He often prayed in the early hours of the day (Mk 1:35).
      2. He was known to pray all night (Lk 6:12).
      3. He prayed before making major decisions (Lk 6:12-13).
      4. The Spirit enabled Jesus to pray with great power and will enable us to pray like Him.
   C. Being filled with the Spirit will transform your prayer life.
      1. Read Romans 8:26-27 and Jude 1:20.
      2. According to these passages, when we are filled with the Holy Spirit, we receive a prayer language that engages heaven and allows us to pray at a level which exceeds our vocabulary.
      3. Such prayer builds our faith.

II. **AUTHENTIC PENTECOSTALISM CAUSES THE BELIEVER TO WALK IN THE SUPERNATURAL POWER OF GOD.**
   A. The Pentecostal church should be a church of power.
      1. If we are authentic Pentecostals, miracles will follow our ministries (Mk 16:14-19).
   B. When a person is baptized in the Holy Spirit, he or she will supernaturally speak in other tongues (Ac 2:4).
      1. Note how *they* spoke the words the Spirit gave them.

      2. Other evidences of the power of the Spirit are witnessing, love for one another, love for the Word, power for Christian living, miracles, signs, and wonders.
  C. Unlike other powers, Pentecostal power is unlimited---because it is God's power.

III. AUTHENTIC PENTECOSTALISM PRODUCES PEOPLE WHO ARE DETERMINED TO PERSEVERE.
  A. Early believers were filled with the power of the Spirit and faithfully served Christ in the face of great opposition.
  B. Consider the perseverance of the twelve apostles.
      1. According to church history all of them except for John were martyred for the gospel.
      2. Men like Paul faced constant and great opposition, but by the power of the Spirit they persevered (Col 1:29).

IV. AUTHENTIC PENTECOSTALISM WILL PERPETUATE ANOTHER GENERATION OF PENTECOSTALS.
  A. The early church knew how to perpetuate another generation of Pentecostals.
      1. The apostles made sure the new believers in Samaria received the gift of the Spirit (Ac 8:17-18).
      2. Paul's first question to the 12 believers in Ephesus "Did you receive the Spirit when you believed?" (Ac 19:1-2).
  B. There must be a rebirth of Pentecost in every generation.
  C. It is our responsibility to pass on authentic Pentecostalism to our children.

Conclusion and Altar Call
1. God has provided a way for us to become authentic Pentecostals and demonstrate Pentecostal power (Ac 1:8).
2. Let us come and be filled with the Spirit.
3. We will then go out and proclaim the gospel in the power of the Spirit.

[DN]

Speaking in Tongues and the Baptism in the Holy Spirit

Sermon in a Sentence: If you will ask, the heavenly Father will give you the gift of the Holy Spirit evidenced by speaking in tongues as the Spirit gives utterance.

Sermon Purpose: That believers will be filled with the Spirit and understand the purpose and nature of speaking in tongues.

Texts: Acts 2:1-4; 17-18

Introduction
1. Just before Jesus returned to heaven He commanded His disciples to wait for the Holy Spirit (Ac 1:4-5).
2. They received the Spirit and spoke in tongues as the Spirit gave the ability (Ac 2:4).
3. Peter stood to explain the experience (Ac 2:17-18).
4. He said that this experience is for all believers (Ac 2:38-39).
5. This message will address four issues concerning the experience of speaking in tongues:

I. **WHAT IS SPEAKING IN OTHER TONGUES?**
   A. Speaking in tongues is not...
      1. ... a spiritual status symbol.
      2. ... a shortcut to spiritual maturity.
      3. ... something that causes us to go into a trance or hypnotic state.
   B. Speaking in tongues is Holy Spirit-inspired speech in a language not known to the speaker.

II. **ARE TONGUES STILL IN OPERATION TODAY?**
   A. All over the world millions of believers are being filled with the Spirit with the biblical evidence of speaking in tongues.
   B. Nevertheless, some teach that tongues have ceased.
      1. They use 1Co 13:8-10 to teach this, saying that "that which is perfect" is the completed canon of Scripture.
      2. However, "that which is perfect" is referring to the second coming of Christ.
      3. Until Jesus comes again people will need all of the charismatic gifts, including speaking in tongues.

III. **HOW DOES SPEAKING IN TONGUES OPERATE TODAY?**
   A. The Bible describes three manifestations of tongues:
      1. Tongues as an evidence (Ac 2:4; 10:46; 19:6).
      2. Tongues as intercessory prayer (Ro 8:26-27).

        a. The Spirit prays through us "with groans that words cannot express" (v. 26).
        b. He prays according to the will of God.
    3. Tongues as a spiritual gift (1Co 12:10).
        a. They are to be used with the gift of interpretation of tongues to communicate a divine message to the church.
        b. We can learn about the proper use of this gift in 1 Co 14:1-32.

IV. SOME QUESTIONS THAT PEOPLE ASK ABOUT SPEAKING IN TONGUES TODAY:
   A. Were tongues given to the church so we can preach the gospel in a foreign language?
      1. No, they are rather the sign that someone has been empowered by the Spirit to be Christ's witness (Ac 1:8).
   B. Are tongues always human tongues?
      1. No, they are sometimes in a human language and sometimes in an angelic language (1Co 13:1).
   C. Did Jesus speak in tongues?
      1. We don't know, the Bible does not say.
      2. We do know, however, that Jesus did pray in the Spirit (Lk 10:21-22; Jn 11:33).
   D. Are tongues to be feared?
      1. Jesus taught that there is nothing to fear (Lk 11:13).
      2. The baptism in the Holy Spirit is a wonderful gift from God to be welcomed and cherished, and not to be feared.

Conclusion and Altar Call
   1. Don't be satisfied until God fills you with His Spirit.
   2. The Father will give the Holy Spirit to those who will ask for the gift (Lk 11:9-10; 13).
   3. Come now to be filled with the Holy Spirit.

[DWC]

80. What It Means To Speak In Tongues

Sermon in a sentence: Each time we are filled with the Spirit and speak in tongues we should remember what it means.

Sermon purpose: That believers might be filled and refilled with the Spirit evidenced by speaking in tongues, and that they might better understand the meaning of the experience.

Text: Acts 1:12-18, 31-33

Introduction
1. As Pentecostals we believe in speaking in tongues.
   a. But, have you ever asked yourself what it means to speak in tongues?
   b. The Jews asked this very question when they heard the 120 disciples speak in tongues on the Day of Pentecost (v.12).
2. Peter answers this question in our text.
3. According to him speaking in tongues means at least four things:

I. **SPEAKING IN TONGUES MEANS THAT THE BIBLE IS TRUE** (vv. 16-17, 33).
   A. The Bible is true because God keeps His promises (v. 16).
   B. The Bible is true because it was God who spoke through the prophets (v. 17b).
   C. The Bible is true because it is practical (v. 33).
   D. Speaking in tongues gives evidence that the Bible is valid for today.

II. **SPEAKING IN TONGUES MEANS THAT TIME IS SHORT** (v. 17a).
   A. Time is short because the outpouring of the Holy Spirit marked the beginning of the last days.
      1. We have already spent over 730,000 of the last days (the approximate time from Pentecost until today).
      2. This means that the coming of the Lord is very close.
   B. Speaking in tongues reminds us that we do not have time to waste.
      1. We must preach the gospel in all the world before Jesus comes again (Ac 1:8; Mt 24:14).

III. **SPEAKING IN TONGUES MEANS THAT EACH OF US CAN BE USEFUL IN THE CHURCH** (vv. 17b-18).
   A. We can all be useful because God empowers and uses everyone to accomplish His purposes.
      1. He empowers and uses both men and women (vv. 17-18).

      2. He empowers and uses both young and old (v. 17d).
  B. Everyone who speaks in tongues can be useful in the church.
      1. Because everyone who speaks in tongues has been baptized in the Spirit and empowered to do God's work.
      2. Therefore, all should seek the baptism of the Holy Spirit.

IV. SPEAKING IN TONGUES MEANS THAT JESUS IS ALIVE
(vv. 31-33).
  A. We know that Jesus is alive…
      1. … because His grave is empty (vv. 31-32).
      2. … because He is at the right hand of God (v. 33a).
  B. Further, we also know that Jesus is alive because He poured out the Holy Spirit at Pentecost (v. 33b).
      1. And He is still doing it today.
      2. And He is still doing it in the same way, that is, evidenced by speaking in tongues and Spirit-empowered witness.
  C. You, too, can be filled with the Spirit today.
      1. You will speak in tongues.
      2. You will become Christ's witness.

Conclusion and Altar Call
  1. Anytime we are filled or refilled with the Spirit and speak in tongues we remember that…
      a. … the Bible is true and we can trust its promises.
      b. … time is short, therefore, we need to get busy proclaiming Christ to the lost both at home and to the nations.
      c. … we have each been empowered and gifted by the Spirit and are, therefore, useful in the work of God.
      d. … that Jesus is alive, and He will help and protect us as we serve Him.
  2. Come now to be filled with the Spirit.

[FK]

Section 4

The Importance of Pentecost

81. The Acts 1:8 Church

Sermon in a Sentence: We need to be an Acts 1:8 Church, that is a church that is full of the Spirit and focused on reaching all people with the gospel.

Sermon Purpose: To see people filled with the Spirit and commit themselves to God's mission to reach all people and nations.

Text: Acts 1:8; 11:19-21; 13:1-3

Introduction

1. In Acts 1:8 Jesus gave clear instructions to His disciples.
2. God wants His church to be an Acts 1:8 Church, that is, a church that is empowered by the Spirit and actively witnessing to all tribes and people groups.
3. A significant word in Acts 1:8 is the word "and": "You will be my witnesses in Jerusalem *and* in all Judea *and* Samaria, *and* to the end of the earth."
   a. Jesus did not say "then" but "and."
   b. The implication is that we reach all groups simultaneously,
4. In this message we will present the churches in Jerusalem and Antioch as models of Acts 1:8 Churches.

I. THE ACTS 1:8 PATTERN IN THE JERUSALEM CHURCH

A. The Jerusalem church was slow to become a true Acts 1:8 Church.
  1. Acts chapters 2-7 show the Jerusalem church being filled with the Spirit.
     a. However, they were slow to go to the Gentiles.
     b. They focused almost entirely on the Jews.
  2. God, however, allowed persecution to come, which helped them reach out to the Samaritans (Ac 8:1-5).

B. Discrimination against Gentiles hindered the Jerusalem church from quickly becoming an Acts 1:8 Church.
  1. At first those who left Jerusalem due to persecution preached to Jews but not to Gentiles (Ac 11:19).

C. It required a divine intervention to move the church into ministry to the Gentiles. (Story of Cornelius, Acts 10:1-46).
  1. Peter's attitude toward unclean animals was indicative of the overall attitude of Jews toward Gentiles (Ac 10:9-15).
  2. The church in Jerusalem was initially resistant when they heard that Peter had crossed the barrier to minister to Gentiles (Acts 11:1-3).

D. Finally, a few years after Pentecost, a group of men broke the cycle and began to intentionally preach to Gentiles in Antioch (Ac 11:20).

II. THE ACTS 1:8 PATTERN IN THE ANTIOCH CHURCH
A. In contrast to the Jerusalem church the Antioch church *quickly* became a true Acts 1:8 Church.
   1. Many Gentiles were saved in Antioch when believers began to preach to them (Ac 11:20-21).
   2. Barnabas and Saul spent a year teaching and strengthening the church (Ac 11:22-26).
   3. Soon after its birth the Antioch church became the first church to intentionally send missionaries to the Gentiles (13:1-3).
   4. As a result, the gospel began to rapidly spread to the nations
   5. The rest of the book of Acts is focused on the mission to the Gentiles.
B. How did the church in Antioch become a real Acts 1:8 Church?
   1. It was a church that recognized people based on their ministry rather than their ethnicity (Ac 13:1).
   2. It was a Spirit-filled church.
      a. There were prophets and teachers (Ac 13:1).
      b. The Spirit spoke through prophecy as the church was fasting and seeking God in prayer (Ac 13:2).
   3. It was a church that listened and took responsibility to obey God's command to take the gospel to the nations (Ac 13:3).
      a. When we read that the church laid hands on them and sent them off it means that the church took upon itself the responsibility to support them both in prayer and finances.

III. THE ACTS 1:8 PATTERN IN OUR CHURCH TODAY
A. Today God is calling us to be a true Acts 1:8 Church.
B. Like the church in Antioch we must do the following:
   1. We must seek God in prayer and be filled with the Spirit.
   2. We must hear and accept God's clear command to commit ourselves to His mission.
   3. We must not just fulfill the command halfway by only reaching our Jerusalem and Judea, but we must obey Christ and take the gospel to all tribes and nations in the power of the Spirit.

Conclusion and Altar Call
1. Let us come now and commit ourselves to God's mission
2. And let us be filled with the Spirit to accomplish the task.

[JK]

82. Christ's Priority for the Church

Sermon in a Sentence: Jesus' last words show His priority that we be filled with the Spirit and take the gospel to the whole world.
Sermon Purpose: That people be filled with the Spirit and witness.
Text: Acts 1:8

Introduction
1. Just before Jesus ascended, He explained His priority (Ac 1:8).
2. His priority is not establishing a political kingdom but saving lost souls through Spirit-empowered preaching (vv.6-8).
3. These important last words of Jesus speak to us about two persons, a promise, a purpose, and a program:

I. TWO PERSONS TO FOCUS ON
A. Acts 1:8 focuses our attention and our lives on our relationship with two people: Christ and the Holy Spirit.
   1. Jesus said we are to be *His* witnesses through the indwelling power of the *Holy Spirit*.
   2. Christ gives us our mission, and the Holy Spirit gives us power to accomplish the mission.
B. We serve God the Father as we relate to Christ and the Spirit.
   1. The Father has put Christ as the head of the Church; we must therefore obey Him (Eph 1:22, Jn 14:15, 21).
   2. Together, the Father and Christ have sent the Spirit to be the dynamic presence and power in the Church (Jn 14:23,26; Ac 2:33).
   3. Therefore, the church must stay focused on obeying Christ and living in the Spirit.
      a. Christ is in us and we are in Him through the Spirit (Jn 14:16-18,19).
      b. Through an intimate relationship with the Spirit we remain connected to Christ.

II. A PROMISE TO FULLY RECEIVE
A. Christ promised that His disciples would receive the Holy Spirit and be filled with power to serve God.
   1. This is the Father's promise (Ac 1:4-5).
   2. This promise is of vital importance.
   3. Jesus spoke about it often (Jn 7:38-39; 14:16-17; 20:21-22).
B. On the Day of Pentecost God fulfilled the promise (Ac 2:4).
C. Jesus said that the promise of the Spirit is for all Christians of all times (Jn 7:38).

1. On the Day of Pentecost Peter stated that the promise is for everyone (Ac 2:38-39).
2. If you will ask in faith, you will be filled with God's power just like the disciples in the book of Acts.

III. A PURPOSE TO FULFILL
A. Christ's mission to save the world is the eternal purpose of God.
  1. There is no greater purpose to live for.
  2. Therefore let us fully commit ourselves to Christ's mission.
B. While the baptism in the Holy Spirit brings great blessing into the believer's life, its primary purpose is to empower us to serve Christ's mission to preach the gospel.
  1. Just as Christ's mission has not changed, neither has His purpose for giving us the gift of the Spirit (Mt 24:14).
  2. Just as the disciples in Acts needed the Spirit to accomplish the task of preaching the gospel, we also need the Spirit's power.
  3. This is why Jesus told them not to leave Jerusalem until they had received the Spirit's power (Ac 1:4).
  4. The task is too big to accomplish in our own power.

IV. A PROGRAM TO FOLLOW
A. Jesus told His disciples that they were to begin preaching in Jerusalem.
  1. However, they were not to stop there.
  2. They were to expand their ministry into Judea and Samaria, and to the ends of the earth.
B. This program was to be outward focused, reaching out to those who had not yet heard the gospel.
C. Christ's program has not changed.
  1. We have a responsibility to preach in our own Jerusalem and Judea (that is, our own home area).
  2. Further, we must always be expanding the preaching of the gospel outward ("to Samaria and to the ends of the earth"), that is, to other areas, cultures, and nations that have not received the gospel.

Conclusion and Altar Call
1. Will you accept Christ's priority for the Church and for your life?
2. Come and be filled with the power of the Spirit and become part of His mission.

[MT]

83. Don't Throw Out the Baby With the Bath Water

Sermon in a Sentence: The excesses seen in Pentecostalism must not cause us to reject the true work of the Spirit in our lives.
Sermon Purpose: That believers will open their lives to the true work of the Spirit and be filled with the Spirit today.
Text: Acts 1:4-8; 2:1-4

Introduction
1. Today many are disappointed with what they see in Pentecostalism.
    a. They see the excesses of some.
    b. And they observe the wrong emphasis of others.
    c. As a result they are tempted to walk away from the work of the Holy Spirit in their lives.
2. Americans have a saying that applies to this situation:
    a. They say, "Don't throw out the baby with the bath water."
    b. This could be restated, "Don't throw out what is good and precious with what has been soiled and dirtied."
    c. In our disgust with the negative things going on in the name of Pentecostalism, we must not throw out what is real and true—the true work of the Spirit in our lives.
3. Our text tells the story of the first outpouring of the Spirit on the church on the Day of Pentecost.
    a. It set a pattern for the church of every age until Jesus comes again.
    b. It represents true Pentecostal experience.
    c This story will help us if we understand what true Pentecostalism is, but first let's discuss …

I. WHAT TRUE PENTECOSTALISM IS NOT
  A. It is not just a style of worship.
    1. Though we Pentecostals often practice enthusiastic worship, true Pentecostalism is much more than that.
    2. It is a powerful encounter with a living God.
  B. It is not just a seeking after new experiences.
    1. Although we as Pentecostals seek and cherish fresh experiences with God, true Pentecostalism is more than seeking after the newest "spiritual experience."
    2. Our experiences must be solidly based on New Testament precedent.
  C. It is more than speaking in other tongues.
    1. Although we Pentecostals firmly believe in speaking in tongues, true Pentecostalism is much more than this.

      2. Speaking in tongues is the sign of a greater inner reality (Ac 2:4).

II. WHAT TRUE PENTECOSTALISM IS
   A. It is a significant daily relationship with the Holy Spirit.
      1. The Holy Spirit is not a power or an influence, He is a divine person—He is God!
      2. We can have daily fellowship with Him (2Co 13:14).
   B. It is a submitting to the whole of Scripture.
      1. Pentecostals are people of the Book, that is, the Bible.
      2. Everything we believe and do must be based solidly on Scripture.
   C. It is supernatural power for living.
      1. The Holy Spirit empowers us to live the life of Christ.
      2. It is a life characterized by compassion, holiness, and power.

III. THE PRIMARY PURPOSE FOR PENTECOST
   A. According to Jesus, the primary purpose of Pentecost is empowerment for witness (Ac 1:8).
   B. That empowerment comes through a powerful, life-changing experience that Jesus called the baptism in the Holy Spirit (Ac 1:4-5).
   C. The great news is you can be empowered by the Spirit today (Lk 11:9-13).

Conclusion and Altar Call
   1. So, let's don't throw out the baby with the bath water.
   2. Come now and experience the reality of the Holy Spirit in your life.

[JP]

84 | God's Answer Comes By Fire

Sermon in a Sentence: The only answer to a world in crisis is the fire of the Holy Spirit empowering Christians and convincing people to follow Christ.

Purpose: To see people filled with the Holy Spirit and empowered to witness.

Text: 1 Kings 18:18-40

Introduction

1. In the time of Elijah, God's people were going through a great crisis.
   a. It was a *material crisis:* They had abandoned God, and, as a result, He had stopped the rain resulting in famine.
   b. It was a *spiritual crisis:* They had abandoned God for idols.
   c. Today, our society--and even many believers in the church--are experiencing a spiritual crisis, just like Israel at that time.
2. In our Bible story Elijah's answer came by fire.
   a. The same is true today, the answer to our problems will come by the fire of the Holy Spirit.
   b. We thus learn four important lessons from the story of Elijah:

I. SPIRITUAL CRISIS COMES WHEN MAN ABANDONS GOD.
   A. Israel had abandoned the one true God to serve Baal and Ashera.
      1. Their worship involved idolatry and sexual immorality.
   B. The names have changed, but these god's are still worshiped today.
      1. In our society idolatry and free sex are still rampant.
      2. The church needs God's power to convince the world to leave this situation and serve the one true God.
      3. Only the fire of the Spirit can bring the answer.

II. WE CANNOT SERVE TWO GODS AT THE SAME TIME.
   A Israel was vacillating between two ideas (v. 21).
      1. They were vacillating between Baal and Yahweh.
      2. That is, between false and true, light and darkness, superstition and truth.
   B. Neither can we serve two masters.
      1. When we waver we cause others to stumble.
      2. God has promised His Spirit for those who, like Elijah, stand firm.

III. GOD'S ANSWER COMES BY FIRE (v. 24).
  A. In Scripture, fire is a symbol of God's presence:
     1. God manifested Himself to Moses by fire (Ex. 3:2).
     2. God guided Israel by a pillar of fire (Ex 13:21; Nu 14:14).
     3. The fire of God consumed Israel's sacrifice (Lev 9:23-24).
     4. John said that Jesus would baptize believers with the Holy Spirit and fire (Lk 3:15).
     5. Tongues of fire appeared over the believers at Pentecost (Ac 2:3).
     6. Here in our text fire from God came and consumed Elijah's sacrifice (1 Kg 18:38).
  B. When the fire falls, men are changed and the Holy Spirit brings revelation, purity, freedom from sin and slavery, and power to fulfill the mission of God.
  C. We need this fire today more than ever in order to fulfill God's mission.
     1. We need it to be freed from bondages, from sin and vice, from idolatry, and from the pleasures of the world.
     2. When this fire from God comes into your life, you will not be the same.
     3. We need the fire of God!

IV. WE MUST PREPARE OURSELVES FOR THE FIRE.
  A. Elijah repaired the altar of the Lord (1Kg 18:30).
     1. We are God's temple, indwelt by God's Spirit (1Co 3:16-17, 6:19).
     2. We must repair the altar of our hearts by repenting of our sins and surrendering our lives to God (Ac 2:38).
  B. Elijah then prayed to God (1Kg 18:36).
     1. Prayer is vital to preparing us to receive the fire of God.
     2. God sends His Spirit in response to earnest prayer.
  C. After Elijah prayed, the fire fell from heaven.
     1. In the same way God will send the fire of the Spirit from heaven.
     2. He will cleanse you and fill you with His power.

Conclusion and Altar Call
  1. Come, place yourself on God's altar.
  2. Commit yourself to His mission and His will and get ready to experience the fire of His Spirit.
  3. Let us believe that God will fill us with His Spirit today.

[SOA]

85. It's A Supernatural World

Sermon in a Sentence: God wants to work supernaturally in your life today.

Sermon Purpose: That believers will be baptized in the Holy Spirit and experience the supernatural power of God.

Text: 1 Corinthians 2:1-5

Introduction
1. In our text Paul describes his ministry as one marked by the supernatural.
2. He describes it the same way in other places (2Co 12:12; Ro 15:18-19).
3. Just as supernatural power was at work in Paul's life and ministry, the power of the Holy Spirit should be at work in our lives and ministries today.
4. Let's look at how the power of the Spirit is a central part of every step of our lives in Christ.

I. **THE SPIRIT'S POWER IS MANIFESTED WHEN WE ARE SAVED.**
   A. Look at some of the things the Spirit did in your life when you were saved.
      1. You were powerfully born of the Spirit (Jn 3:3-7),
      2. He powerfully raised you from spiritual death unto life (Eph 2:1, 4-5).
      3. He powerfully rescued you from the dominion of Satan (Col 1:13).
      4. Through His power He made you a new creation in Christ (Tit 3:5; 1Co 6:11b; 2Co 5:17).
      5. He supernaturally sealed you and included you in Christ (Eph 1:13; 1Co 12:13).
   B. We must conclude that your new birth was supernatural from the beginning to the end.
      But there's more….

II. **THE SPIRIT'S POWER IS MANIFESTED IN OUR SANCTIFICATION.**
   A. When Christ saved you, the Spirit sanctified you (1Co 6:11).
      1. That is, He made you holy.
      2. He set you apart for God's exclusive use.
   B. Listen to what the Spirit did for you:
      1. By His power He separated you to live a holy life (Ac 26:18; 2Th 2:13).

    2. By His power He caused you to become more like Jesus (1Jn 2:6; 2Co 3:18).
    3. And now, by that same power He reminds you that you are God's child (Ro 8:16).
  C. Think of it, the power of the Spirit is working in you right now! *But there's more….*

III. THE SPIRIT'S POWER IS MANIFESTED WHEN WE ARE BAPTIZED IN THE HOLY SPIRIT.
  A. He will empower you to live a victorious life (Gal 5:16; Ro 8:13).
  B. He will empower you to be an effective witness for Christ (Ac 1:8).
  C. He will empower you for gifted ministry (1Co 12:8-10).

Conclusion and Altar Call
1. Now ask yourself three important questions:
   a. Do I believe God is a God of the supernatural?
   b. Do I believe God is working the same today as He always has?
   c. Do I believe Him enough to take Him at His word and be filled with the Spirit today?
2. Then, come now and be filled with His Spirit.
   a. Ask in faith (Lk 11:9, 13).
   b. Receive by faith (Lk 11:10; Mk 11:24).
   c. Speak in faith (Ac 2:4).

[JP]

86. Needed: Spirit-Empowered People

Sermon in a Sentence: The life and ministry of Moses illustrate how all of God's people need to be filled with the power of the Holy Spirit.

Sermon Purpose: To motivate church members and leaders to seek the Spirit and His power to finish the mission of God.

Text: Numbers 11:1-6; 10-17; 24-29

Introduction
1. The church's great need is for Spirit-empowered people.
2. We can learn important lessons from the life of Moses about the need for God's people to be empowered by the Holy Spirit:

I. **GOD'S MISSION CAN NEVER BE ACCOMPLISHED IN HUMAN STRENGTH ALONE** (Nu 10:33; 11:1-15).
   A. Difficult circumstances will come (Nu 11:1-9).
      1. God uses these things to test and build our faith in Him.
      2. Our tendency is to be carnal, unspiritual and ungrateful.
         a. We quickly forget what God has done in the past.
         b. We are often contaminated and discouraged by other people's lack of faith (Nu 11:4).
   B. Moses became discouraged and wanted to quit (vv. 10-15).
      1. Imagine how Moses felt when he heard the multitudes crying for him to give them what they wanted.
      2. Consider carefully Moses' words.
      3. We must be Spirit-led to deal with carnal people.
   C. However, note how Moses dealt with his discouragement.
      1. He took the problem to God in prayer (Nu 11:11a).
      2. Spirit filled people deal with problems in spiritual ways.
      3. God's response to Moses is His answer to the need of His people and the key to success for the church.

II. **GOD'S ANSWER IS A SPIRIT-EMPOWERED COMMUNITY RATHER THAN ONE ANOINTED PERSON** (Nu 11:16-17).
   A. Instead of telling Moses to get tough and persevere, God put His Spirit on 70 others to help him.
   B. We learn several important lessons from this:
      1. No one leader is meant to do everything himself/herself.
      2. The answer is not to just have more leaders, but rather more Spirit-empowered leaders.
      3. We must resist the temptation to put people in leadership who are not Spirit-filled.
      4. If there is a lack of Spirit filled people, we should focus on leading people into receiving the Spirit.

- C. However, notice that it was Moses' desire that not only leaders have the Spirit, but that *all* of God's people be empowered by the Spirit.
    1. God later revealed His plan and promise (Joel 2:28-29).
    2. And yet Moses already realized that this was what all the people needed.
- D. Moses was, himself, empowered by the Holy Spirit, and this made all the difference in his life (Nu 11:17a).
    1. Moses failed when working on his own (Ex 2:11-15).
    2. Now Moses was being led by the supernatural power of God's Spirit.
- E. Moses did not make the mistake of proudly thinking he was the only person God could use (Nu 11:26-29, note v. 29).
    1. He realized that people need the Spirit's power to accomplish God's mission for their lives.
    2. We can do nothing right (live, work, pray, lead, etc.) without the power of the Spirit.
- F. Since Pentecost, what Moses longed for, and what Joel prophesied, is now possible (Ac 1:4-5, 8; 2:17-18).
    1. The gift of the Spirit is for everyone (Ac 2:38-39).
    2. The power of the Spirit is the key for the church to finish the mission of preaching the gospel to the whole world.

III. THE GREAT NEED OF THE CHURCH TODAY IS SPIRIT-EMPOWERED PEOPLE.
- A. If we work to see people filled with the Spirit, the Church will go forward in power and will finish the task of reaching the nations with the gospel.
- B. God is looking for people like Moses, people who will be moved by a passion to see all God's people filled with the Spirit and used in the ministry of proclaiming the gospel.
    1. If Africa is to be saved we must dedicate ourselves to teach, preach and pray for people to receive the Spirit.
    2. We must determine to work until every member has been filled with the Spirit.

Conclusion and Altar Call
1. God knows you need the Holy Spirit, and He has promised that He will fill you.
2. Come in faith today and receive.

[MT]

87 Passion and Power: The Spirit's Gift to the Church

Sermon in a Sentence: The Holy Spirit will give us passion and power to reach the nations.
Sermon Purpose: To see people filled with the Spirit's power and passion to see the nations saved.
Text: Acts 1:8

Introduction
1. Jesus commissioned His church to preach the gospel to all nations and peoples before He returns from heaven (Mt. 24;14).
2. Like Jesus, the Holy Spirit is passionate to see every tribe, tongue, people, and nation come to know and serve God.
3. To ensure that the gospel will reach all people, Jesus has poured out the Holy Spirit upon His disciples to empower them for worldwide evangelism.
4. We need to understand four important truths about how the Spirit gives to us passion and power for God's mission.

I. THE HOLY SPIRIT IS PASSIONATE FOR ALL PEOPLE.
   A. Jesus has assured us of success; we will reach the "ends of the earth with the gospel (v.8b).
   B. To ensure that success He has promised us His power (v.8a).
   C. This power includes both power and passion for the lost (Examples: Ac 4:8,13,20,31).

II. THE HOLY SPIRIT USES DISCIPLES TO REACH THE NATIONS.
   A. Spirit-filled disciples are the Spirit's *primary resource* for reaching the nations.
   B. The disciples' *primary purpose* is to participate with the Spirit in the work of redeeming the nations.
   C. The disciple's *primary role* is to proclaim the message of Christ in the power of the Spirit.

III. THE HOLY SPIRIT GIVES POWER TO REACH ALL NATIONS.
   A. The Holy Spirit is the divine orchestrator of God's plan for worldwide evangelism.
   B. If the church is to successfully execute that plan, God's people must be empowered by the Spirit.
      1. Power to accomplish the task is essential to the success of any endeavor.

2. Holy Spirit empowerment is at the center of God's plan to redeem the nations.
3. The aim of this empowerment is to enable the church to effectively reach the lost through anointed preaching of the gospel.

IV. THE HOLY SPIRIT GIVES PASSION AND POWER FOR US TODAY.
A. The promise of the Spirit is for all of God's people in every place until the end of the age.
   1. It is still good today (Ac 2:38-39).
   2. It is ours for the asking (Lk 11:1, 13).
B. The gift of the Spirit is the same today as it was in the New Testament.
   1. The power of the Spirit for the church is the same.
   2. The passion of the Spirit for the nations is the same.
C. We must each be filled with the Spirit's power and passion to reach the nations before Jesus comes again.

Conclusion and Altar Call
1. Being filled with the Spirit results in us experiencing the passion and power of the Holy Spirit!
2. Come and experience the Spirit today.

[JE]

88 The Primacy of Pentecost

Sermon in a Sentence: Like Jesus and the early church, we must emphasize the primary importance of the baptism in the Holy Spirit in our lives and churches.

Sermon Purpose: To encourage believers and churches to emphasize Pentecost in their lives and ministries and to call believers to be baptized in the Holy Spirit today.

Text: Acts 1:1-8

Introduction
1. In recent years there has been a decrease in Pentecostal experience and practice in our churches.
2. We must honestly ask ourselves, "Have we as a movement lost our passion for Pentecost?"
3. This message will address this important subject.
4. We will ask, "How does our passion for Pentecost stack up with that of Jesus and the apostles?"
5. Let's first look at how Jesus and the apostles viewed Pentecostal experience:

I. **THE PRIMACY OF PENTECOST IS DEMONSTRATED IN THE MINISTRY OF JESUS** (Note these seven amazing facts).
   A. Jesus did not begin His ministry until He was first anointed by the Holy Spirit (Lk 3:21-23).
      1. His baptism in the Holy Spirit resulted in Spirit-anointed ministry (Lk 4:1, 14).
   B. The anointing of the Holy Spirit was the central theme of Jesus' inaugural address (Lk 4:17-18).
   C. Jesus taught His disciples how they, too, could be filled with the Spirit (Lk 11:9-13).
   D. Jesus' last sermon before His crucifixion was filled with teaching about the coming of the Holy Spirit (Jn 14:12-17, 26; 15:26; 16:13-15).
   E. Jesus' first act after His resurrection was to breath on His disciples and say, "Receive the Holy Spirit" (Jn 20:21).
   F. Jesus' last command before returning to heaven was to order His disciples to wait for the coming of the Spirit (Lk 24:49, Ac 1:4-5).
   G. Jesus' final promise to His church was a promise of the Spirit's power (Ac 1:8).

II. **THE PRIMACY OF PENTECOST IS DEMONSTRATED IN THE MINISTRY OF PETER** (Note these three significant facts).

    A. Peter's first sermon is full of teaching about the work of the Spirit (i.e., Acts 2:17-18; 33; 38-39).
    B. Peter's second sermon in Acts also contains an allusion to Pentecost (Ac 3:19).
    C. Peter's sermon in Caesarea talks about the Spirit's power (Acts: 10:38) and resulted in the Spirit being poured out.

III. THE PRIMACY OF PENTECOST IS DEMONSTRATED IN THE ACTION OF THE APOSTLES IN SAMARIA (ref., Ac 8:4-17).
    A. There was a missing ingredient in the Samaritan revival.
        1. Many were saved, healed, and delivered from demons.
        2. But none were being filled with the Spirit (vv. 4-13).
    B. The apostles viewed the situation with alarm, so they sent Peter and John to remedy the situation (vv. 14-17).

IV. THE PRIMACY OF PENTECOST IS DEMONSTRATED IN THE MINISTRY OF PAUL (Note these three facts).
    A. Paul's first concern upon arriving in Ephesus was to see the twelve disciples filled with the Spirit (Ac 19:1-10).
    B. Paul's continuing concern for the Ephesian church was that it remain full of the Spirit (Eph 5:18).
    C. Paul's first concern in his last message to Timothy was to ensure that he remained full of the Spirit (2Ti 1:6).

V. HOW SHALL WE RESPOND TO THESE TRUTHS?
(We must ask ourselves three probing questions).
    A. Why were Jesus and the apostles so passionate about Pentecost?
        1. It is the believer's primary means of living an effective Christian life.
            a. The Christian life from beginning to end is a life lived by the power of the Spirit (Gal 3:3).
        2. It is the church's primary means of fulfilling the Great Commission (Ac 1:4-8).
    B. How does our passion for Pentecost stack up with that of Jesus and the apostles?
    C. What are we going to do about it?

Conclusion and Altar Call
    1. Let's commit ourselves to teaching and preaching the message of Pentecost.
    2. Lets come and receive the power of Pentecost today.

                                                            [DRM]

89. Why Receive the Holy Spirit?

Sermon in a Sentence: Many benefits come into our Christian lives once we have been filled with the Holy Spirit.
Sermon Purpose: That believers will be baptized in the Holy Spirit.
Text: Ephesians 5:15-20

Introduction
1. In this passage Paul urges believers to "be filled with the Spirit."
2. There are at least seven scriptural reasons each of use should be filled or refilled with the Spirit today:

I. **WE HAVE BEEN COMMANDED TO RECEIVE THE SPIRIT.**
   A. In our text Paul commanded believers to be filled with the Spirit (Eph 5:18).
   B. Jesus also commanded believers to be filled with the Spirit (Lk 24:49; Ac 1:4-5).

II. **THE HOLY SPIRIT HAS BEEN APPOINTED AS OUR TEACHER.**
   A. Effective teachers mentor others through the relationships they build.
      1. The Holy Spirit has been sent as each believer's instructor and mentor (Jn 14:26).
   B. When we receive the Holy Spirit…
      1. He heightens our awareness of the will of God.
      2. He heightens our sensitivity to the voice of God.
      3. He opens to us the word of God.

III. **THE HOLY SPIRIT HAS BEEN APPOINTED AS OUR GUIDE.**
   A. A guide is one who knows the way.
      1. The Holy Spirit is such a Guide (Jn 16:13-15).
   B. The Holy Spirit sometimes guides us through revelation.
      1. He knows the Father's will and reveals it to us.
      2. He guides us in ministry (Ac 13:1-4).

IV. **THE HOLY SPIRIT EMPOWERS US FOR SERVICE.**
   A. Jesus needed the Spirit's power to perform His ministry (Lk 4:17-18; Ac 10:38).
   B. Paul needed the Spirit's power to perform his (2Co 3:2-6).
   C. If Jesus and Paul needed the Spirit's empowerment, so do we (Jn 15:5; Ac 1:8).

V. THE HOLY SPIRIT WILL PRAY THROUGH US WHEN WE DO NOT KNOW WHAT TO PRAY FOR.
A. The Spirit will enhance our prayer lives (Ro 8:26-27).
B. He will anoint us to pray in our own native language and in languages He gives to us (1Co 14:15).

VI. THE HOLY SPIRIT WILL BE OUR COMFORTER (Jn 15:26).
A. The Greek word translated "Comforter" (KJV) is *paraklete.*
   1. It means "one called alongside to help."
B. As our Paraklete,
   1. The Spirit is our Intercessor before God.
   2. The Spirit is a constant abiding presence in our lives.
   3. The Spirit will assist us in every situation.
C. To receive maximum assistance from the Heavenly Father we must each be filled with the Holy Spirit.

VII. THE HOLY SPIRIT WILL CONVICT US OF SIN.
A. One work of the Spirit is to convict sinners of their sin and draw them to Christ (Jn 6:44; 16:5-8).
B. The Spirit also works in believers' hearts to convict them when they stray from the path.
C. It is, therefore, important that we be filled with the Spirit and that we walk in the Spirit each day of our lives (Gal 5:16, 24-25).

Conclusion and Altar Call
Come now and be filled with the Spirit

[DN]

90 Strengthening Our Pentecostal Heritage

Sermon in a Sentence: We as Pentecostals must not lose our heritage as God's Spirit-empowered people.
Sermon Purpose: That believers may be filled with the Spirit and commit themselves to remaining truly Pentecostal in experience and practice.
Text: Psalm 85:6

Introduction
1. We as Pentecostals have been given a great heritage.
2. We trace our heritage back to Acts 1:8 and 2:4.
3. We must hold fast to this Pentecostal heritage.
4. We must pray like the Psalmist: "Will you not revive us again, O Lord?" (Ps 85:6).
5. Let's look at this great heritage:

I. WE HAVE A GREAT PENTECOSTAL HERITAGE.
  A. Our Pentecostal heritage began on the Day of Pentecost.
   1. The disciples waited and the power came (Ac 2:1-4).
   2. The baptism in the Holy Spirit, evidenced by speaking in tongues and resulting in empowered witness, is our beautiful Pentecostal heritage (Ps 16:6).
  B. The apostles passed on the heritage of Pentecost.
   1. They passed it on at Samaria (Ac 8:17-18).
   2. They passed it on at Caesarea (Ac 10:44-46).
   3. They passed it on at Ephesus (Ac 19:1-16).
  C. The power of Pentecost was lost during church history.
   1. The church lost its emphasis on the work of the Spirit.
   2. Though there were awakenings from time to time, there was nothing like the experience of the early church.
  D. In these last days the power of Pentecost has been restored.
   1. It started with the Azusa Street Revival in Los Angeles, California, USA, in 1906 and in other places.
   2. Eventually it spread to Africa.
   3. It is now spreading across the continent.
  E. We must never forget that the power that came at Pentecost and Azusa can be received by us today.

II. WE MUST NOT ABANDON THIS HERITAGE.
  A. In recent years we have seen our Pentecostal heritage weakened.
   1. Sadly, we have begun turning from our heritage.
   2. We have tried to become like others.

B. This weakening of our Pentecostal heritage has weakened our churches.
      1. Remember, this power that has come can also go.
         a. For example, look at Sampson (Jdg 16:20).
      2. Have we become empty voices?
   C. We must stop playing with our Pentecostal heritage.
      1. We must stop rationalizing the Spirit out of our midst.
      2. We must stop importing false teachings into our churches.
      3. We must revive our churches (Rev 3:2; Ps 119:28).

III. **THINGS WE MUST DO TO STRENGTHEN OUR PENTECOSTAL HERITAGE.**
   A. We must once again reverence the Word of God.
   B. We must live holy lives.
   C. We must respect our truly Pentecostal leaders and the people of God.
   D. We must revive true Pentecostal preaching.
   E. We must revive our evangelistic zeal.
   F. We must "Pentecostalize" our Bible Schools.
   G. We must contend for our Pentecostal faith (Jude 3).

Conclusion and Altar Call
   1. Our Pentecostal heritage is the emphasis on the empowering of the Holy Spirit.
   2. If we lose our heritage we will lose our souls.
   3. We must keep the fire of Pentecost burning in our lives, families, churches.
   4. Come now and be filled and refilled with the Spirit.

[JI]

SECTION 5
CONFERENCE LESSONS

91 The Holy Spirit and the Mission of God

Sermon in a Sentence: God's mission is to redeem all nations, and He sent His Spirit to empower us to take the message of Christ to the nations.

Sermon Purpose: That the hearers will better understand the mission of God and the role of the Holy Spirit in fulfilling God's mission.

Text: Acts 1:1-8

Introduction
1. This lesson will answer two important questions:
   a. What is the mission of God?
   b. What is the role of the Holy Spirit in fulfilling that mission?

I. **WHAT DO WE MEAN BY THE TERM "MISSION OF GOD?"**
   A. The mission of God (sometimes called the *missio Dei*) can be defined as God's purpose and work in the world in relation to mankind.
      1. God's purpose is to redeem and call unto Himself a people out of every kindred, tongue, people, and nation on earth (cf. Rev. 5:9).
      2. This mission includes "all the world" and "every nation" (Mt. 24:14).
      3. God's mission is moving toward a definite climax: "The kingdoms of this world are become the kingdoms of our Lord, and of his Christ; and he shall reign for ever and ever" (Rev. 11:15).
   B. From the beginning it has been God's plan to redeem all nations.
      1. God created Adam (and thus all humankind) in His own image (Ge 1:27); therefore, God has a loving interest in all mankind (Jn 3:16).
      2. When Adam sinned, all of mankind fell with him (Ge 3:6; Ro 5:12); therefore, all people need a Redeemer (2 Co 5:14-15).
      3. God promised to bless "all nations" through the seed of Abraham (Ge 12:3), that is, through Jesus the Redeemer (Ga 3:16).
      4. The entire Bible reveals and elaborates on this plan.
   C. As "God's missionary people" we have been called to join God in His mission (Jn 20:21-22).

II. THE MISSIONARY NATURE OF GOD
A. When we think of missions, we often think of the Great Commission.
 1. Read Mt. 28:18-20 (cf. Mk 16:15-16; Lk 24:46-49).
 2. As important as this is, our understanding of God's mission must go much deeper.
B. God by His very nature is a missionary God, and because He is a missionary God…
 1. … He created humankind in His own image.
 2. … He gave the Bible to reveal Himself to mankind.
 3. … He raised up and called Israel to be a light to the nations.
 4. … He sent His Son, Jesus, to die for the sins of all people of all nations (2Co 5:15; 1Jn 4:14).
 5. … He sends His church into the world to preach the good news to all nations (Jn 20:22).
 6. … He sent His Spirit to empower His church to witness to all nations before Christ comes again (Lk 24:46-49)

III. THE HOLY SPIRIT IS A MISSIONARY SPIRIT.
A. This fact is seen throughout Scripture:
 1. It is seen in the ministry of Jesus (Lk 4:17-18; 10:38).
 2. It is most clearly seen in the book of Acts (Ac 1:8).
B. If we as God's missionary people are to effectively participate in God's mission, we, and every member of our churches, must be empowered by the Spirit.
 1. Jesus' two final mandates:
    a. To preach to all nations (Ac 1:8b).
    b. To be empowered by the Spirit (Ac 1:8a).
 2. Our missionary task concerning the Holy Spirit:
    a. Get a clear understanding of the missional purpose of the baptism in the Holy Spirit (Ac 1:8).
    b. To personally experience the Spirit's power.
    c. To preach and teach effectively on the work of the Spirit in empowering the church to complete the mission of God.

Conclusion and Altar Call
Let's commit ourselves to be personally empowered by the Spirit and to lead our churches to be empowered by the Spirit in order to effectively advance the mission of God at home and around the world.

[DRM]

92 Spirit Baptism Revisited

Sermon in a Sentence: If we are to complete the Great Commission, we must stop neglecting Spirit baptism and begin to emphasize it again until every believer is filled with the Spirit.

Sermon Purpose: A call to the church to revisit and reemphasize this neglected experience. Also, a call to properly understand Spirit baptism's purpose as being empowerment for missional witness.

Text: Acts 1:8

I. THE PURPOSE OF SPIRIT BAPTISM
A. Acts 1:8 clearly reveals that the purpose of Spirit baptism is to empower believers for effective witness.
B. Acts shows us the effect of Spirit baptism in action.
C. The gift of the Holy Spirit is available to every believer to empower them as witnesses for Christ (Ac 2:38-39).

II. A PROBLEM: SPIRIT BAPTISM NEGLECTED
A. Statistics indicate a waning emphasis on Spirit baptism in the Africa Assemblies of God.
B. This is a serious problem…
   1. … since the purpose of Spirit baptism is empowerment to fulfill the Great Commission.
   2. … since fewer and fewer of our people are being filled with the Spirit.
   3. Question: How will we effectively reach the lost if we fail to emphasize this experience?
C. A number of things could be causing this alarming situation:
   1. A change in focus from God's mission to our prosperity.
   2. Pressure to look evangelical and mainstream.
   3. A tendency to depend on human effort rather than the power of the Spirit
D. Let us not be foolish like the Galatians (Gal 3:1-5).
   1. If we ignore the gift of the Holy Spirit, we are ignoring the very power of God to save the world.
   2. In light of the *purpose* and the *problem*, we must begin to emphasize Spirit baptism once again.

III. A PLEA TO EMPHASIZE SPIRIT BAPTISM
A. We must experience a fresh outpouring of the Spirit.
   1. For this to happen, we must…
      a. … begin to seek the gift in prayer.
      b. … begin to regularly preach and teach on the subject.

  c. … encourage every person in our churches to receive the Spirit.
 2. A Pentecostal church cannot survive without revival.
 B. All of Scripture calls us to emphasize Spirit baptism:
  1. The Old Testament anticipated the need for the Spirit's empowerment and prophesied the experience for all believers (Nu 11:25-29; Zec 4:6; Joel 2:28-29).
  2. In the gospels Jesus modeled, promised, and commanded Spirit baptism (Mt 12:28; Lk 3:21-22; 4:1-2, 14-19; 24:49; Ac 1:4-8).
  3. In Acts and the epistles the early church experienced and emphasized Spirit baptism for all (Ac 2:38-39, 8:15-17, 19:1-6).
 C. Some today say that Spirit baptism was only for the early church.
  1. They don't understand the purpose of the experience.
  2. The early church needed the Spirit to be powerful witnesses for Christ.
  3. We need the Spirit today for the same reason.
 D. The need of the world today calls us to emphasize Spirit baptism.

IV. A PLAN TO HELP US REFOCUS ON SPIRIT BAPTISM
 A. We must *become convinced of the need* to return to a regular emphasis on this neglected experience.
 B. We must *commit ourselves to personally* seek the continual fullness of the Spirit in our own lives
 C. We must *commit ourselves to prayer* for the outpouring of the Spirit and a growing vision for God's mission.
 D. We must *commit ourselves to preach and teach* regularly about the Holy Spirit and missions.
 E. We must *commit ourselves to being witnesses* in the power of the Holy Spirit.

Conclusion and Altar Call
 1. Let us come and seek to be refilled with the Spirit.
 2. And let us commit ourselves to helping all believers receive the power of the Spirit and begin to witness for Christ.

[MT]

93. What it Means to Be Pentecostal

Sermon in a Sentence: We must all commit ourselves to being truly Pentecostal as presented in the book of Acts.

Sermon Purpose: That Christians will commit themselves to becoming truly Pentecostal, and that they will lead others to do the same.

Introduction
1. What is your vision of Pentecostalism?
2. There are competing visions of what it means to be Pentecostal:
   a. Personal blessing Pentecostals.
   b. Backward-looking Pentecostals.
   c. Praise and worship Pentecostals.
   d. Domesticated Pentecostals.
   e. Spectator Pentecostals.
   f. Post-Pentecostals
   g. Authentic Pentecostals
3. Let's look in Acts to find a definition of authentic Pentecostalism.
   a. Acts is not just a history book.
   b. It is the Pentecostal's manual for life and practice.
   c. Biblically defined, authentic Pentecostalism is *a popular, last-days, Spirit-empowered missionary movement.*
4. To be truly Pentecostal means four things:

To be truly Pentecostal means that
I. WE PROCLAIM THE SAME MESSAGE AS DID THE CHURCH IN THE BOOK OF ACTS.
   A. At the heart of true Pentecostalism is a message—the gospel.
      1. That is, the message of Jesus.
      2. In the book of Acts this is sometimes called the *kerygma.*
         a. The Greek word meaning "proclamation."
         b. That is, the content of the preaching in Acts.
   B. Early Pentecostals called it the "Full Gospel" (Four pillars:)
      1. Jesus saves.
      2. Jesus heals.
      3. Jesus baptizes in the Holy Spirit.
      4. Jesus is coming again.
   C. Sadly, many so-called Pentecostals today are compromising the gospel.

To be truly Pentecostal means that
II. WE SHARE THE SAME MISSION WITH THE CHURCH IN THE BOOK OF ACTS.

- A. That mission is most clearly stated in Acts 1:8: "You will be my witnesses to the ends of the earth."
- B. Three deeply-held beliefs drove early Pentecostals to the ends of the earth preaching the gospel:
  1. Jesus could come at any moment.
  2. We have been commissioned to reach the nations with the gospel before He comes again.
  3. Pentecost gives us the power we need to get the job done.

To be truly Pentecostal means that

III. WE EMBRACE THE SAME EXPERIENCES AS DID THE CHURCH IN THE BOOK OF ACTS.
- A. Pentecostalism is a rebellion against dead orthodoxy.
- B. What experiences do we find in the book of Acts?
  1. The new birth as a powerful life-changing experience.
  2. Holiness of life.
  3. Encounters with God.
  4. The defining experience—the baptism in the Holy Spirit.
- C. How Pentecostals define Spirit-baptism:
  1. A powerful spiritual experience for all believers …
  2. … separate from salvation …
  3. … whose purpose is empowerment from mission …
  4. … and is evidenced by speaking in tongues.
- D. This doctrinal formulation has catapulted the Pentecostal church around the world.

To be truly Pentecostal means that

IV. WE UTILIZE THE SAME METHODS AS DID THE CHURCH IN THE BOOK OF ACTS.
- A. Discuss: "What made the early church so successful?"
- B. They used the following methods:
  1. Powerful Spirit-anointed proclamation of the gospel.
  2. A demonstration of God's power and presence through signs following.
  3. The establishment of Spirit-empowered missionary churches.

Conclusion and Altar Call
1. Are you really Pentecostal?
2. Do you desire to be?
3. Let's commit ourselves to being authentically Pentecostal.

[DRM]

94. Pentecost and the Next Generation

Sermon in a Sentence: The experience of the baptism in the Holy Spirit must be passed on to our youth and children.
Sermon Purpose: To motivate pastors, parents and church leaders to ensure that the next generation is Spirit-filled.
Text: Joel 2:28; Acts 2:17, 38-39

Introduction
1. In a relay race passing the baton is a critical moment which can totally change the outcome of the race.
2. This lesson is about passing the baton of Pentecost.

I. **A PROMISE: FOR YOUNG AND OLD ALIKE** (Joel 2:28; Ac 2:17)
   A. Joel's prophecy and its fulfillment in Acts shows that the gift of the Spirit is for young and old alike.
      1. It includes sons and daughters, young and old.
      2. Acts 2:38-39 clearly shows a generational step.
   B. God wants every believer to receive the Spirit: "I will pour out my Spirit on *all flesh*." that is to say, *all people*" (Ac 2:17).
   C. Jesus said that "the kingdom of God belongs to such as these" (Lk 18:15-16).
      1. If the kingdom of God belongs to children, why would the promise of the Father not be for them?
   D. Children, too, can experience the baptism in the Holy Spirit.
      1. We should teach them about the experience …
      2. … and then pray with them to receive the Holy Spirit.
      3. John the Baptist was filled with the Holy Spirit "even from birth." (Lk 1:15).
      4. While John the Baptist was unique, it is still true that no child is too young to be filled with the Spirit.

II. **A RESPONSIBILITY: TO PASS PENTECOST ON TO THE NEXT GENERATION**
   A. In the history of the church many important truths have been lost for periods of time because they were not passed on.
   B. Read: Deuteronomy 4:9
      1. If we are not careful we can let the power and experience of God's presence "slip from our hearts."
      2. How can we pass on what we have let slip away from our own hearts?
      3. Our responsibility to our children starts with maintaining the vibrancy of our own experience with the Holy Spirit.

    C. Deuteronomy 6:1-2, 7: Moses emphasized the importance of passing on to the next generation the truth of God's word so that our children can also enjoy the blessing and benefits of walking with God.
        1. The home is the most effective place for training children.
        2. Parents have a responsibility to *impress* these things on their children.
    D. We also need to introduce the gift to children who come to church but whose parents are not Christians.
        1. What greater impression could be made on a child than for him or her to experience the power and presence of the Spirit of God?

III. **A WARNING: IF THE NEXT GENERATION IS NOT FILLED WITH THE HOLY SPIRIT PENTECOSTAL CHURCHES WILL DIE.**
    A. We must be intentional about leading our youth and children into the baptism in the Holy Spirit.
        1. Discuss Judges 2:10-13.
        2. Do not think that just because children and young people are in church today this alone will cause them to grow up and serve the Lord faithfully.
    B. If we want to see the next generation involved in God's mission, it needs the power of the Holy Spirit.
        1. Children and youth can be witnesses, even now.
        2. Remember, the primary purpose for the baptism in the Holy Spirit is power for witness (Ac 1:8).

IV. **A PLAN: WHAT WE MUST DO TO PASS ON PENTECOST TO THE NEXT GENERATION.**
    A. We must teach the next generation about the Holy Spirit.
    B. We must pray for the next generation to receive the Spirit.
    C. We must train parents how to teach their children to be filled with the Spirit.
    D. We must make opportunities for the next generation to receive the Holy Spirit.

Conclusion and Altar Call
    1. Let it not be said that our generation failed to lead the next generation into Pentecost.
    2. Come and commit yourself to passing the baton of Pentecost.

[MT]

95 | Women and Pentecostal Revival

Sermon in a Sentence: Women are essential in God's plan to build a Spirit-empowered church, and therefore must get involved.
Sermon Purpose: To motivate women to be filled with the Spirit and to get involved in bringing Pentecostal revival to the church.

Introduction
When it comes to bringing Pentecostal revival to a church...

I. WOMEN ARE IMPORTANT.
A. Throughout Scripture women were important in God's work:
  1. Before Pentecost they were important.
     a. Deborah was a prophetess and a judge in Israel (Jdg. 4:4-15).
     b. Mary conceived by the Holy Spirit (Lk 1:35).
     c. Elizabeth prophesied (Lk 1:41-45).
     d. Mary prophesied (Lk 1:46-55).
     e. Anna prophesied over Jesus (Lk 2:36-38).
  2. Women received the Spirit at Pentecost (Ac 1:14).
  3. Priscilla was a Spirit-empowered minister along with her husband (Ac 18:26).
     a. She led Apollos into the experience of the baptism of the Holy Spirit.
  4. Philip's four daughters were prophetesses (Ac 21:9)
B. Women have been important in the spread of Pentecostalism around the world.
  1. Women shared in leadership at Azusa Street.
  2. Many times women led the missionary charge.
     a. Agnes Osmond was the first person to speak in tongues at the Topeka Outpouring.
     b. Many women went out from Azusa as church planters, evangelists, pastors, and missionaries.
  3. In Burkina Faso 100,000 women pray every Saturday for an outpouring of the Spirit.
C. Women will be essential in bringing Pentecost to Africa.

II. WOMEN ARE NECESSARY.
A. Women represent more than half of the African church.
B. God has given them special gifts and talents:
  1. He has given them determination.
  2. He has given them compassion.
  3. He has given them sensitivity to His Spirit.
C. Women have unique opportunities to share the gospel.
  1. They can go places that are difficult for men.

2. They can talk to each other concerning sensitive issues.

III. WOMEN MUST GET INVOLVED.
A. Women must get a clear (and biblical) understanding of the experience of the baptism in the Holy Spirit.
   1. At Pentecost the women …
      a. … received the same command as the men: "Wait for the Spirit" (Ac 1:4).
      b. … received the same promise of power (Ac 1:8).
      c. … had the same experience (Ac 2:4).
      d. … received the Spirit for the same purpose, that is, to be Christ's witnesses to the lost (Ac 1:8; 2:18-19).
   2. While speaking in tongues has many benefits for the Spirit-filled Christian, it is not the primary purpose for the baptism in the Holy Spirit. The primary purpose of Spirit baptism is power for witness.
B. Women must have a genuine experience with the Spirit.
   1. Come with a sincere desire to better serve Christ.
   2. Leave the desire to be seen behind.
   3. Humble yourselves before God and He will lift you up (1 Pet 5:6).
   4. Know that God will give you the desire of your heart.
C. How can women get involved in bringing Pentecost to Africa?
   1. Understand what the mission of God is (Lk 24:46-49).
   2. Obey Christ's command to be filled with the Spirit.
   3. Take advantage of the opportunities the Lord is giving you to witness for Him.
      a. Don't be afraid if God calls you to preach he will open the door for you and equip you.
      b. Possibly God will call you to a ministry of prayer, or service.
   4. Remember, all have been called to be Christ's witness.
   5. Women of God, let us rise up in the power of the Spirit and be all that Christ has called us to be.

Conclusion and Altar Call
Come and commit yourself to be God's instrument in bringing a Pentecostal revival to your church and to Africa.

[SM]

96 The Pentecostal Bible School

Sermon in a Sentence: Our Bible schools must be truly Pentecostal if the church is to effectively serve God's mission.

Sermon Purpose: That administrators and teachers understand what a Pentecostal Bible school looks like, and then seek to make their schools truly Pentecostal and truly missional.

Text: Matthew 28:19-20, John 14:12, 15-18, 26

Introduction
1. We must ensure that our Bible schools are truly Pentecostal.
2. Four key elements of a truly Pentecostal Bible school:

I. THE MISSION OF A PENTECOSTAL BIBLE SCHOOL
A. We define our mission and goals in order to provide a measuring stick to keep us on track.
B. The primary mission of the Pentecostal Bible school is to help the church to fulfill the mission of God.
C. Goals of the Pentecostal Bible school include the following:
  1. Keeping the church Pentecostal.
     a. Pentecostal educators are "guardians of the faith."
     b. The church must have the Spirit's power to fulfill the mission of God.
  2. Fulfilling the Great Commission.
     a. Training is part of the Great Commission (Mt 28:20).
     b. We must learn to train "Pentecostally."
  3. Keeping the church biblical.
     a. Pentecostal experience and practice must be based solidly on sound interpretation of Scripture.
  4. Producing Christ-like ministers of the gospel.
  5. Multiplying workers for the harvest.

II. THE ETHOS OF A PENTECOSTAL BIBLE SCHOOL
A. "Ethos" refers to the spirit or culture of a community.
B. The Pentecostal Bible school must cultivate a "culture of the Spirit."
  1. The Spirit must be present in every class and activity.
  2. This culture does not happen by chance; it must be deliberately and intentionally created and maintained.
C. The Pentecostal Bible school must also develop a "culture of mission."
  1. Creating a culture of mission requires a clear understanding of and commitment to God's mission.
  2. God "gives the Holy Spirit to those who obey him" (Ac 5:32), that is, those who will get involved in His mission.

3. Without a commitment to God's mission, our training becomes merely academic, and our schools exist merely for the purpose of giving out diplomas and producing "professional" clergymen who are largely ineffective in building God's kingdom.
D. Leaders must create and maintain a culture of the Spirit

III. THE CURRICULUM OF THE PENTECOSTAL BIBLE SCHOOL
A. The school must have a Pentecostal curriculum.
1. "Curriculum" includes everything we do and teach in the school.
2. Curriculum is Pentecostal only if it fully addresses Pentecostal issues.
B. We can "Pentecostalize" our curriculum by addressing the following issues:
1. Does the program emphasize the Holy Spirit?
2. How many courses deal specifically with person and work of the Holy Spirit?
3. Does the curriculum train ministers to be truly Pentecostal in understanding, experience, and practice in the real world?
4. We must move our students into practical ministry.
C. The most important factor in Pentecostal training is the Pentecostal teacher.
1. Curriculum is more than just what is taught from books.
2. The greatest influence on the students comes from the lives of the teachers.
3. Bible schools must have Spirit-filled teachers who understand how to teach and minister the Spirit's power just as Jesus did.

IV. THE SPIRITUAL LIFE OF THE BIBLE SCHOOL
A. The Pentecostal Bible school should be a place where the Spirit of God is manifestly present.
B. Our chapel services should be pervaded by the Spirit's presence and focused on fulfilling God's mission.
1. Spiritual gifts and disciplines must be developed.
2. The atmosphere is pervaded by prayer.

Conclusion and Altar Call
Let's commit ourselves to developing and maintaining truly Pentecostal Bible schools.

[JE]

97 | How to Preach on the Baptism in the Spirit

Sermon in a Sentence: You can preach powerfully and effectively on the baptism in the Holy Spirit.

Sermon Purpose: That ministers and Christian workers may know how to preach effectively on the baptism in the Holy Spirit.

Introduction
1. On the Day of Pentecost Peter preached the first sermon of the Christian era (Ac 2:14-17; 32-33; 37-39; then 47b).
2. Although it was an evangelistic setting, he dealt with the baptism in the Holy Spirit.
   a. 10 of 25 verses (40% of the sermon) deal with the subject.
   b. The same emphasis continued in His second sermon (Ac 3:19-21).
3. This Message: How to preach on the baptism in the Holy Spirit.

I. THE IMPORTANCE OF PREACHING ON THE BAPTISM IN THE HOLY SPIRIT
A. It is true, "you get what you preach for."
B. Some negative consequences of failing to preach effectively on the baptism in the Holy Spirit:
   1. Believers are not filled with the Spirit, thus…
      a. … they are open to attacks of the enemy.
      b. … they are ineffective witnesses.
   2. Church life becomes insipid (salt without savor!).
   3. Mission flounders.
C. Reasons for such neglect:
   1. Lack of understanding and conviction …
      a. … concerning the importance, purpose and nature of Spirit baptism.
      b. … concerning God's mission and our responsibility.
   2. Theological and experiential drift …
      a. … because we no longer believe strongly in Spirit baptism, we don't preach on it.
      b. … because we don't preach on it, few are filled.
      c. … because few are filled, we no longer believe strongly in the experience.
      d. … so we spiral downward away from Pentecostal experience and practice.
   3. Fear of failure: Because pastors fear that people will not be filled, and they will be shamed, they avoid preaching on the baptism in the Holy Spirit.
   4. Lack of competence.

            a. Pastors have never really learned how to effectively preach on the subject and pray with people to receive the Spirit.
            b. So they avoid the subject.
    D. The potential benefits of preaching on Spirit baptism in the context of mission:
        1. Believers will begin to understand, hunger, and be filled.
        2. The church will grow and mature.
        3. The church will be empowered and inspired to get involved in missions.
    E. We are each personally responsible for preaching on the baptism in the Holy Spirit (1 Co 9:16).

II. **HOW TO PREACH EFFECTIVELY ON THE BAPTISM IN THE HOLY SPIRIT**
    A. Our people being filled with the Spirit and empowered as witnesses must become a priority in our thinking.
    B. Three characteristics of an effective sermon:
        1. *Clarity:* You explain clearly what you mean.
        2. *Faith:* You preach believing that God will work.
        3. *Balance:* You balance boldness with humility.
    C. When you preach on the baptism in the Holy Spirit, keep these three goals in mind:
        1. You are trying to *create desire* in people's hearts to be filled with the Spirit (Mt 5:6; Jn 7:37).
        2. You are preaching to *inspire faith* in the hearts of the people to receive the Spirit (Jn 7:38; Ga. 3;2, 14).
        3. You are trying to *give clear understanding* to the people.
            a. Of the experience itself.
            b. Of how to receive the Spirit.
            c. Of what to expect when they come to receive.
    D. Concerning the altar call.
        1. Always give an altar call.
        2. Be positive.
        3. Expect results.

Conclusion and Altar Call
God will use you to guide people into the baptism in the Holy Spirit.

[DRM]

98. Praying With Believers to Receive the Spirit

Sermon in a Sentence: You can effectively in pray with believers to be baptized in the Holy Spirit.

Sermon Purpose: To help Spirit-filled believers know how to help other believers receive the Holy Spirit and to inspire them to pray with others to receive.

I. **PRELIMINARY CONSIDERATIONS**
   A. Who can be filled with the Holy Spirit?
      1. Anyone who has been truly born again.
   B. Who can pray with others to be filled with the Spirit?
      1. Anyone who has been filled with the Spirit.
      2. The chief requirement is simply the desire to see others blessed and used by God.
   C. The proper biblical context for receiving the Holy Spirit:
      1. The seeker should understand and be committed to God's mission (Ac 5:32).
      2. The seeker must be hungry for God (Mt 5:6; Jn 7:37).
      3. The seeker must exercise faith (Gal 3:5; 14).
      4. You must pray. (In Acts the Spirit is always received in the context of prayer.)

II. **THE PROCEDURE: HOW TO PRAY WITH SOMEONE TO BE FILLED WITH THE HOLY SPIRIT** (Three Steps:).
   A. Step 1: The Interview.
      1. Encourage the candidate by saying that he is doing the right thing, and that God is pleased with him.
      2. Inspire the candidate's faith. You could say…
         a. "This will be one of the greatest days of your life."
         b. "God has something very special for you."
      3. Give Instructions with two goals in mind: to inspire expectant faith and to bring clear understanding.
         a. How to inspire expectant faith in the seekers heart:
            1) Tell them what Jesus said: "Ask and it will be given you…" (Lk 11:9, 13).
            2) Say, "This means that when you ask God will give you the Holy Spirit" (Lk 11:9-10).
         b. How to bring the seeker to a clear understanding:
            1) Tell the seeker exactly what you are going to do.
            2) Let the seeker know exactly what to expect.
            3) Example Prayer: *"We will pray two prayers. First we will ask God to fill us with the Holy Spirit. When we do, God will answer, and He will*

give us His Spirit. Next we will take a step of faith and receive the Holy Spirit. We will pray, 'In the name of Jesus I receive the Holy Spirit.' When you pray this prayer, believe in your heart and you will sense His Spirit filling you. Then you will begin to speak as the Spirit inspires in a language you have never learned."

- B. Step 2: Prayer Engagement.
    1. Lead the seeker in asking in faith (Lk 11:9, 13).
        a. Example Prayer: *"Lord I come to be filled with the Holy Spirit...There is nothing I want more...You have promised that everyone who asks, receives...I am asking and I expect to receive...give me the Holy Spirit."*
        b. Then tell him, *"Sense the presence of God coming upon you."*
    2. Lead him in receiving by faith (Lk 11:10; Mk 11:24).
        a. Tell him, *"This is a step of bold faith."*
        b. *"Lord, in Jesus Name, I receive the Holy Spirit."*
        c. *"Now, receive by faith ... Sense the Spirit's presence within."*
    3. Encourage the seeker to speak out in faith (Ac 2:4).
        a. Sense the Spirit's presence within.
        b. Speak from where you sense God's presence!
    4. If necessary, repeat the procedure.
        a. Point out how they may better respond to the Spirit.
- C. Step 3: Post-prayer guidance.
    1. If they are filled with the Spirit, speak to them about ...
        a. Beginning witnessing for Christ immediately.
        b. How their new life in the Spirit must be maintained.
    2. If they are not filled, encourage them by saying,
        a. *"Don't be discouraged. Keep seeking, you will soon be filled. Jesus promised."*
        b. Maybe they would like to pray again.

III. OTHER CONSIDERATIONS.
- A. Learn what the Bible says on the subject by studying the word of God, especially the book of Acts.
- B. Don't be too spiritually lazy to pray with people.
- C. When praying with people to receive, watch your intensity level. Be upbeat and positive but don't be pushy.

Conclusion and Altar Call

There is nothing more satisfying than helping people experience God's Spirit.

[DRM]

99 | Planting Spirit-Empowered Missionary Churches

Sermon in a Sentence: We must be intentional about planting Spirit-empowered missionary churches.

Sermon Purpose: That church planters will know how to plant churches that are full of the Holy Spirit and focused on the mission of God.

Introduction
1. Christ has called us to plant churches.
2. An important question: What kind of churches shall we plant?
    a. Shall we plant weak, dependent churches?
    b. I suggest we plant "Spirit-empowered missionary churches!"
3. Where shall we look for a model?
    a. The book of Acts.

I. THE ACTS MODEL: SPIRIT-EMPOWERED MISSIONARY CHURCHES

A. Acts 1:8 is the key verse of the book of Acts.
   1. This verse suggests two characteristics of the kind of churches Jesus wants planted:
      a. They must be empowered by the Spirit ("You will receive power when the Holy Spirit comes…").
      b. They must be focused on the mission of God: ("And you will be my witnesses…to the ends of the earth").
   2. When we plant churches, we should *intentionally* plant Spirit-empowered missionary churches.
      a. These churches that will soon be able to plant other Spirit-empowered missionary churches.
      b. This strategy will produce a "spontaneous multiplication of churches."
B. We, like Paul, should plant churches in key locations.
   1. Examples: Paul planted churches in Corinth, Athens, and Ephesus (Ac 17:15ff; 18:1ff; 19:1ff).
   2. However, what is the point if the churches we plant do not have the spiritual vitality to reproduce themselves?
C. By planting Spirit-empowered missionary churches we are following the biblical pattern.
   1. Jesus Himself planted such a church (Ac 1:8).
   2. The apostles insisted on planting Spirit-empowered missionary churches.
      a. The apostles concern in Samaria (Ac 8:17-18).
      b. Paul's strategy in Ephesus (Ac 19:1-10).

II. THE IMPORTANCE OF INTENTIONALITY IN PLANTING SPIRIT-EMPOWERED MISSIONARY CHURCHES
   A. We wrongly assume that because we are Assemblies of God we are automatically planting Pentecostal churches.
      1. Or, because the AG is a missionary fellowship we are automatically planting missionary churches.
      2. It is a mistake to think this way.
   B. In planting new churches we must move with "intentionality."
      1. Every decision must be deliberate.
      2. Every action must be intentional.
      3. All must be aimed at producing a predetermined result: A Spirit-empowered missionary church.

III. A STRATEGY FOR PLANTING SPIRIT-EMPOWERED MISSIONARY CHURCHES
   A. Envision the type of church you want to plant:
      1. A church focused on the mission of God.
      2. A church that will plant other churches.
      3. A church empowered by the Holy Spirit.
   B. Take definite steps to ensure that such a church emerges.
      1. A church empowered by the Holy Spirit:
         (Class Discussion: Ask, "What steps should we take to ensure that the church we plant is empowered by the Spirit?")
      2. A church that will soon plant other churches:
         (Class Discussion: Ask, "What steps should we take to ensure that the church we plant will soon be planting other churches?")
      3. A church that is focused on the mission of God:
         (Class Discussion: Ask, "What steps should we take to ensure that our church is involved in the missionary program of the national church?")

Conclusion and Altar Call
Let's go out and start hundreds of Spirit-empowered missionary churches.

[DRM]

100 Leading a Local Church Into Pentecostal Revival

Sermon in a Sentence: It is essential that every church experience Pentecostal revival and get busy winning the lost to Christ.
Sermon Purpose: To encourage pastors to lead their churches into Pentecostal revival and to give them a plan on how to do it.

Introduction
1. A Pentecostal church cannot survive as a truly Pentecostal church without periodically experiencing Holy Spirit revival.
2. In this lesson we will discuss how to bring Pentecostal revival to a church.

I. WHAT IS REVIVAL?
A. Revival is giving renewed life to something dead or dying.
B. People have different ideas of what revival is, such as,
   1. Revival is dancing, singing, shouting, excitement.
   2. Revival is blessing and prosperity.
   3. We often get our definitions from personal experiences.
   4. But we should get our definition from the Bible.
C. The book of Acts describes how the first revivals took place.
   1. Acts 1:8 identifies three essential elements to revival:
      a. Salvation through repentance and faith in Christ
      b. Holy Spirit baptism
      c. Powerful witness
   2. Other evidences of revival include miracles, healings, excitement, lively services, and church growth.
      a. However, salvation, baptism in the Holy Spirit and witness are the essential elements of revival.
   3. Genuine revival will perpetuate itself as long these three essential elements are present and active.

II. AN EXAMPLE OF REVIVAL IN ACTS CHAPTER 2
A. Acts 2 shows believers being filled with the Spirit and beginning to witness.
B. Acts 2:37-47 describes a cycle of continuing revival.
   1. Verses 38-41 imply that those saved were also baptized in the Spirit.
   2. A church that is alive with the power of the Spirit will show other evidences of revival (see Ac 2:42-47).
C. True Pentecostal revival happens as people believe the message about Jesus, are filled with the Spirit, and then go out to preach the gospel to others.

III. THE CONTINUING NEED FOR REVIVAL
A. It is discouraging to work for years and see little or no fruit.
1. In the beginning patience and perseverance are needed.
2. We must always keep in mind, however, that Jesus expects us to bring in a harvest (Jn 4:35).
3. This can happen when we have genuine revival.
B. Without a continual move of the Spirit the church will die.

IV. THE ROLE OF LEADERS IN REVIVAL
A. The life and actions of the leader are crucial in bringing revival to a church.
1. A local church will reflect the spiritual life of the leaders.
2. God places leaders in local churches to raise up Spirit-empowered disciples whom He can use to build His kingdom (Eph 4:11-12).
B. At the top of the list in equipping saints for ministry is leading them into Spirit-baptism and the Spirit-empowered life.

V. PRACTICAL ADVICE TO STIMULATE REVIVAL
A. The Samaritan revival illustrates some practical steps we can take to inspire revival (Ac 8:1-8,12, 14-17, 25).
1. Seek to be a Spirit-filled leader (such as Philip (Ac 6:3-5), Peter (4:8), and Paul (9:-17-18; 13:9).
2. Believe and have faith that revival is possible.
   a. Start right now, no matter what your circumstances.
   b. God can even use difficult times to bring revival, as was the case in Acts 8:1-4.
3. Boldly proclaim Christ to the lost (vv. 4-5).
   a. Revival does not come if all we do is preach to the saints.
4. Trust God to confirm the preaching of Christ with signs following (vv. 6-7).
5. Emphasize the need for Spirit baptism and give people the opportunity to receive (vv 15-17).
6. Be an example of the true purpose for Spirit baptism by being a witness yourself (v. 25).

Conclusion and Altar Call
1. Determine that you are going to work to see a true Pentecostal revival come to your church.
2. Let's begin now by coming and asking the Lord to fill us again with His Holy Spirit to empower us for this task.

[MT]

Sermon Text Index

Old Testament	**Sermon Number**
Numbers 11:1-6, 10-17	86
Numbers 11:16-17	56
Numbers 11:24-29	86
Numbers 11:26-29	39
Judges 3:10-11	25
1 Kings 18:18-40	84
Psalm 85:6	90
Joel 2:28	94
Joel 2:28-29	23, 25, 31
Joel 2:28-31	26
Isaiah 10:27	40
Zechariah 4:1-14	57

New Testament

Matthew 12:2-28	38
Matthew 28:18-20	47
Matthew 28:19-20	96
Mark 16:15-16	47
Luke 3:16	4, 17
Luke 11:9-13	6, 16, 69
Luke 24:46-49	47
Luke 24:49	3
Luke 24:45-49	51, 56
John 1:29-34	18
John 4:10-14	32
John 7:37-39	20, 32, 36
John 14:12	48, 96
John 14:15-18	96
John 14:16	70, 72
John 14:12-20	8
John 15:26	70, 96
John 16:7	8

Sermon Number

John 16:7-8	70
John 16:7-15	50
John 20:21-22	29, 47
Acts 1:1-8	21, 38, 60, 66, 88, 91
Acts 1:4-5	5, 12, 25, 27
Acts 1:4-8	1, 3, 26, 30, 44, 47, 83
Acts 1:8	2, 8, 12, 15, 19, 28, 42, 55, 58, 61, 62, 64, 81, 82, 87, 92
Acts 1:1-11	52
Acts 1:12-18, 31-33	80
Acts 2:1-4	2, 26, 33, 35, 37, 58, 59, 64, 78, 79, 83
Acts 2:4	30
Acts 2:1-12	10, 55
Acts 2:14-18	78
Acts 2:17	94
Acts 2:17-18	79
Acts 2:14-41	49
Acts 2:17	43
Acts 2:17-18	31, 67
Acts 2:33	27
Acts 2:38-39	94
Acts 2:1-46	53
Acts 3:1-10	63
Acts 3:19	34
Acts 4:23-31	24, 46
Acts 5:3-4	50
Acts 5:17-20, 29	46
Acts 6:1-5a	65
Acts 8:1-5	54, 65
Acts 8:14-17	3
Acts 8:26-29	65, 77
Acts 8:39-40	65
Acts 10:34-47	22
Acts 11:19-21	81
Acts 13:1-3	81
Acts 13:2	50
Acts 19:1-7	3, 14
Acts 19:1-12	11
Acts 21:8-9	65, 67
Romans 8:1-17	75
Romans 8:1-39	74

Sermon Number

1 Corinthians 1:26-29	45
1 Corinthians 2:1-5	85
1 Corinthians 12:8-11	71
1 Corinthians 14:18	68
2 Corinthians 3:5-6	41
2 Corinthians 3:7-10	7
Galatians 3:2-3	76
Galatians 5:25	73, 76
Ephesians 5:15-20	89
Ephesians 5:18	5
2 Timothy 1:6-8,11-12,14	13

Other Decade of Pentecost Books available from the Acts in Africa Initiative

Power Ministry: How to Minister in the Spirit's Power (2004) (also available in French, Portuguese, Malagasy, Kinyarwanda, and Chichewa)

Empowered for Global Mission: A Missionary Look at the Book of Acts (2005)

From Azusa to Africa to the Nations (2005) (also available in French, Spanish, and Portuguese)

Acts: The Spirit of God in Mission (2007)

In Step with the Spirit: Studies in the Spirit-filled Walk (2008)

The Kingdom and the Power: The Kingdom of God: A Pentecostal Interpretation (2009)

Experiencing the Spirit: A Study of the Work of the Spirit in the Life of the Believer (2009)

Teaching in the Spirit (2009)

Power Encounter: Ministering in the Power and Anointing of the Holy Spirit: Revised (2009) (also available in Kiswahili)

You Can Minister in God's Power: A Guide for Spirit-filled Disciples (2009)

The Spirit of God in Mission: A Vocational Commentary on the Book of Acts (2011)

Proclaiming Pentecost: 100 Sermon Outlines on the Power of the Holy Spirit (2011) (Soon to be available in French, Spanish, Portuguese, and Swahili)

Globalizing Pentecostal Missions in Africa (2011)

The 1:8 Promise of Jesus: The Secret of World Harvest (2012)

All of the above books are available from

AIA Publications
1640 N. Boonville Drive
Springfield, MO, 65803, USA
E-mail: ActsinAfrica@agmd.org

© 2011 AIA Publications
A Decade of Pentecost Publication

NOTES

NOTES

NOTES

NOTES

NOTES

—NOTES—

NOTES

NOTES

NOTES

NOTES

NOTES

NOTES